The Story of
Jewish Holidays and Customs

By the Same Author

A CHILD'S HISTORY OF THE HEBREW PEOPLE

A CHILD'S HISTORY OF JEWISH LIFE

A HISTORY OF JEWISH LIFE IN MODERN TIMES

THE STORY OF MODERN PALESTINE

The Story of
Jewish Holidays and Customs

FOR YOUNG PEOPLE

by

DOROTHY F. ZELIGS

Illustrations by Emery I. Gondor

NEW YORK
BLOCH PUBLISHING COMPANY
"The Jewish Book Concern"
1951

TO THE MEMORY OF

MY MOTHER

BETTY MIRKIN ZELIGS

"Her children rise up and call her blessed"

CONTENTS

	PAGE
INTRODUCTION	xi
BEFORE THE STORY BEGINS	1
Something about Calendars	
ROSH HASHONOH	15
YOM KIPPUR	32
SUKKOS	45
THE SABBATH	67
HANUKAH	95
THE JEWISH HOME	110
Bar Mitzvah	
PURIM	126
PASSOVER	149
SHOVUOS	173
OTHER FASTS AND FEASTS	191
THE JEWISH HOLIDAYS ON PARADE	215
BLESSINGS USED THROUGHOUT THE STORY	226
In English and Hebrew	
INDEX	237

LIST OF ILLUSTRATIONS

	PAGE
Egyptians Inventing the First Solar Calendar	4
Babylonians and the Lunar Calendar	4
The Development of the Hebrew Calendar	10
Shofar-Blowing on Rosh Hashonoh	16
Shofar-Blowing in Ancient Times	21
The Call of Selichos	26
Blessing on the Eve of Yom Kippur	34
Decorating the Sukkah	47
Guarding the Crops	50
The Esrog and the Lulov	56
Lighting the Sabbath Candles	70
Kiddush	73
Gathering the Manna	75
Getting Ready for the Sabbath	79
The Ark with the Torah Scrolls	83
Havdoloh	87
The Re-dedication of the Temple	99
Lighting the Hanukah Candles	104
The Talis and Tefillin	116
Haman Leading Mordecai through the Streets of Shushan	134

PAGE

The Megillah 142

At the Seder 153

Opening the Door for Elijah 160

"An Only Kid" 162

The Exodus 166

Preparing for Passover 168

Moses at Mt. Sinai 175

Harvesting the Grain in Ancient Palestine 177

Confirmation 187

Akiba Teaching the Torah Secretly 204

Planting Trees on Hamisho Osor B'Shevat 211

Blessing of the New Moon 222

INTRODUCTION

The Story of Jewish Holidays and Customs is planned
for children of about nine to eleven years of age, for use in
the intermediate grades. Because of its story form, it is
also suitable for general reading, outside the classroom.
The book describes the observance of Jewish holidays and
customs in an American Jewish family. The historical
significance of the holidays is explained and their meaning for present day Jewish life is brought out.

Since religious observances and ceremonials appeal pri-
marily to the emotional and spiritual side of life, it is especially important that this type of subject matter should
be presented, not on a cold, factual basis, but as a living,
functioning part of Jewish life. The story form is therefore particularly well-fitted for the treatment of this material, since it makes possible a warm and realistic portrayal
of how the members of a family actually participate in
the Jewish life of home and synagogue. The young reader
can identify himself with the characters in the story and
thus enter imaginatively into the atmosphere of each holiday described.

The author has dealt chiefly with the large body of
material which is common to all three major groups in

Jewish life today. However, where certain observances are clearly Orthodox, Conservative, or Reform, these distinctions are fully explained in an objective way, so that children of all groups will be informed about them.

Through the reminiscences of the father in the story, the children are also given a glimpse of the picturesque ceremonial Jewish life as it was lived a generation or two ago, in one of the characteristic Jewish communities of Europe. Some of the new present-day observances in Palestine are also described. Thus, the reader gets a sense of the continuity and development of Jewish life from the past to the present.

The holidays are treated in chronological order except for the minor ones, which are grouped together. This sequence seems especially suitable as Rosh Hashonoh occurs near the beginning of the school year, and many of the holidays will thus be taught as they occur in the calendar year. The study of the Sabbath was placed so that it would come in the school year at a period when there would be less likelihood of its being interrupted by a major holiday. This consideration also determined the placement of other material dealing with observances and customs apart from the holidays. The last chapter in the book is a review of all the holidays.

No effort was made to include all the ceremonials of Jewish life. The selection of material was made on psychological considerations of what is suitable for children of this age level on the basis of their interests and comprehension. Thus, ceremonials associated with the newborn, with marriage, and with death, were omitted. These should be studied in a more advanced grade.

Each chapter is followed by *Things to Do and Talk About*. These classroom aids consist of questions reviewing the story, topics for class discussion, and a variety of suggested activities. A complete dramatization of the Sabbath story is included.

A section in the back of the book, *Blessings Used Throughout the Story,* contains the blessings associated with Jewish ceremonies and customs, in both English and Hebrew.

Since many schools are already using workbooks or activity books in connection with other subjects in the curriculum, it was thought best not to duplicate this technique for the teaching of Jewish holidays. Furthermore, the activities for teaching this subject grow so naturally out of the treatment of the material in the book, that the only further guidance which seems necessary is supplied by the suggestions given at the end of each chapter.

D. F. Z.

The Story of
Jewish Holidays and Customs

BEFORE THE STORY
BEGINS

Something About Calendars

VER since the beginning of the world, the days have been marching steadily across the face of the earth. How difficult it would be if we had no way of keeping count of these days.

Try to imagine what your life would be like if all the calendars suddenly disappeared from the world and there was no way of replacing them. It would be hard to make plans for a certain time in the future, or to remember on what day of the past certain events occurred. Birthdays and holidays might easily get lost. Of course, we could still tell the seasons of the year, but we wouldn't know just when to expect the arrival of the next season. We would very likely say as one poet did, "If winter comes, can spring be far behind?"

And yet, there was a time in the history of the world when there were no calendars. For calendars had to be invented by man. It took a long time to develop the calendars we have today and to make them so exact.

A calendar, as you know, helps us to keep count of the

days. What causes day and night? You have probably learned that the earth is constantly turning 'round and 'round. That part of the earth which faces the sun is having day, and the other part, which is in darkness, is having night. It takes twenty-four hours for the earth to make one complete turn, so one day and night together equal twenty-four hours. At the same time that the earth is turning 'round and 'round, it is also moving slowly around the sun. It takes three hundred and sixty-five days for the earth to move completely around the sun. That is why a *sun-year* is three hundred and sixty-five days long.

The various seasons of the year are caused by the position of the earth as it moves around the sun. We are having summer when our part of the earth is closest to the sun and gets its rays most directly.

The Earth and the Moon

While the earth is turning 'round and 'round and at the same time traveling slowly around the sun, it has a close companion. That companion is the moon. The moon travels around the earth. It takes twenty-nine and a half days for the moon to make one complete trip around the earth. Therefore a *moon-month* is either twenty-nine or thirty days long.

These facts are interesting, but what do they have to

do with calendars? What do they have to do with Jewish holidays? We shall see.

Three Kinds of Calendars

There are three kinds of calendars which are in use in the world today. One kind is based on the sun. It is called a *solar* calendar, from the Latin word *solaris,* meaning *sun*. How long is a *solar* or sun-year?

Another kind of calendar is based entirely on the moon. It is called a *lunar* calendar, from the Latin word *luna,* meaning *moon*.

A third kind of calendar is based on both the sun and the moon.

Solar Calendars

The ancient Egyptians were one of the earliest peoples to invent a calendar. They were the first to base their calendar on the sun. They had a solar year of three hundred and sixty-five days. So you see, the calendar which is most commonly used in the world today, which we shall call our *everyday* calendar, is also a solar calendar. It came to us from early Egyptian days. The ancient Romans and the Christians also helped to develop this calendar, as you shall learn. But its length has remained the same.

Lunar Calendars

The ancient Babylonians, too, were among the first ones to invent a calendar. Theirs was based on the lunar month. They were the first to arrange the months so that the first

day of the month would be the first day of the new moon. Therefore some of their months were twenty-nine days long and others were thirty days long. Can you tell why?

In our *everyday* calendar, the months are not lunar months. The arrangement of the months in this calendar came down to us from the Romans. In the Jewish calendar, however, the months are true lunar months. That means that the first day of every month occurs on the day of the new moon. However, the Jewish calendar is not entirely a lunar calendar, as you shall see.

An interesting example of a present-day calendar which is entirely a lunar one is the calendar of the Mohammedans. A lunar year of twelve months is three hundred and fifty-four days. That is eleven days shorter than the solar year of three hundred and sixty-five days.

Do you know what happens with the Mohammedan festivals? Each year they occur eleven days earlier than the year before, according to the solar calendar. The result is that the same holidays do not always come at the same seasons of the year. Wouldn't it seem strange to us if we celebrated Hanukah in summer on some years? That's what would have happened if the Jewish calendar had remained strictly a lunar one.

A Lunar-Solar Calendar

The Jewish calendar is a combination of the lunar and solar methods of counting time. Let us see how it developed from ancient times. Our Jewish holidays today are based on this Jewish calendar which came down to us from the past.

How the Jewish Calendar Began

The ancient Hebrews, who were shepherds in the vast spaces of the Arabian desert, needed some way to mark the passing of time and to keep track of special days. As other nomadic peoples have done, they chose the moon as the chief guide for their calendar. It was natural for them to do so, for they were very much aware of the moon. On some nights, the brilliant moonlight made the desert bright as day, and at other times, the absence of the moon filled the night with fears and dangers. As they sat outside their tents at the end of the day, the nomads could see the faint new crescent moon. They watched it grow larger each day until it reached the fullness of its splendor and made the desert brilliant with its light. Then they saw it wane day by day, until it seemed to disappear from the sky. They counted the number of days from one new moon to the next. They found that it took twenty-nine and a half days. This period of time they called *one moon*. Our word *month* comes from *moon*. They might have said, "In three moons we will leave this oasis and move to another spot where the grass is more green." Or perhaps they said, "On the fifth day of the new moon we will have a special feast." The moon was their calendar.

How the Jewish Calendar Developed

Later on, the Hebrews settled in the land of Canaan and led an agricultural life. They continued to count their holidays from the first day of the new moon. But the seasons of the year were more important to them, now that they were farmers. Their agricultural festivals were connected with seed-time and harvest. So they had to consider the solar year, too, in their calendar. If they didn't, they would be celebrating Sukkos in the middle of winter on some years. Wouldn't that be a strange time for a harvest festival! Probably, in early times, an extra month was added to certain years by the king, or high priest, or a council of rabbis, to keep the holidays in the right seasons. Finally this was done permanently by adding an extra month to the Jewish calendar either every two or every three years. During these leap years, the Jewish calendar has thirteen months instead of twelve. So you see the Jewish calendar is made up of lunar months, but the number of months is determined by the solar system.

Numbering the Years

Ancient peoples used various ways of numbering the years. Often some important event was used as a starting point. They might have said, "Twenty-five years after the Terrible Earthquake," or, "Forty years after the Great Battle." Frequently years were numbered according to the reign of the kings of the country. The Bible often uses this method of counting years, such as, "In the fifth year of the reign of Josiah."

The Jewish calendar goes back a long, long time in the numbering of its years. It goes back even further than the time of Abraham. In fact, it begins with the date which was believed to mark the creation of the world.

Our *everyday* calendar begins the numbering of its years much later, with the birth of Jesus. This was, of course, begun by the Christians. If you want to know what year it is according to the Jewish calendar, add 3760 years to the date of this year on the *everyday* calendar.

Rosh Hodesh

All the Jewish holidays are figured according to the ancient Jewish calendar. The day begins in the evening, after sunset, when three stars can be seen if the day is clear. That is why the Sabbath and holidays start on the eve of the day before. Their observance is begun at sunset.

The first day of each month is considered a minor holiday and is observed with special prayers and ceremonies. It is called *Rosh Hodesh,* Head of the Month. Rosh Hodesh is the day of the new moon.

It is interesting to know how the Hebrews in ancient times decided which day was the day of the new moon. It had to be either the twenty-ninth day of the month or the thirtieth, because, as you have learned, a lunar month is twenty-nine and a half days. Of course, Rosh Hodesh couldn't start in the middle of a day. All the holidays were counted from the day of the new moon and it would be very confusing if some of the people observed Rosh Hodesh on the twenty-ninth day and others on the thirtieth. So this is what they did. When the end of the moon-month was at hand, people scanned the heavens eagerly for the first signs of the pale, new, crescent moon. Anyone who caught the first glimpse of it hurried to bring the news to the Sanhedrin, the great council of rabbis who made and explained the laws for the Jewish people. The testimony of two reliable witnesses that they had seen the new moon was necessary. The Sanhedrin then announced the date of Rosh Hodesh. The announcement was carried throughout the country and neighboring lands by the lighting of

signal fires on the hilltops. There were certain hills where bonfires were all ready to be lit and where men were stationed to await the signal.

Later, however, bonfires were considered unreliable, and messengers were used instead. Naturally, it took these messengers a long time to reach lands that were distant from Palestine. So the Sanhedrin ruled that Jews living outside of Palestine should observe festivals for two days instead of one, so that they would be sure to include the right day. But Yom Kippur, being a fast day, only had to be kept one day. And that is how the custom of keeping some of our holidays for two days began, way off in ancient times.

Orthodox and Conservative Jews still continue this custom. Reform Jews, however, keep only one day. This means that Rosh Hashonoh and Shovuos are observed for one day by Reform Jews. On the long festivals, Passover and Sukkos, they keep the first and last days as full holidays.

In Palestine, it was never the custom to keep holidays for more than one day because the people always knew the exact day of Rosh Hodesh. So in that country, Jews still observe one day, except for Rosh Hashonoh, which is kept for two days.

When the Jewish calendar was put down in writing, in the fourth century, the days of Rosh Hodesh were decided on permanently.

The Jewish Holidays

Almost all the Jewish holidays that we celebrate today, began a long, long time ago. Most of them were observed by our ancestors in biblical days. Instructions for observing these holidays are given in the Bible and are explained more fully in the Talmud.

Most of the Jewish holidays are based on important

events that occurred in the history of our people in ancient times. Some of the holidays also bring back to our minds how the Jews lived in ancient times, when they were an agricultural people in Palestine. Many of our customs began in those days. We could not understand Jewish life today if we did not know about the past.

It is interesting to think that the holidays which we observe today date back so many hundreds of years. These days help to make up the unbroken chain of Jewish life which reaches from the past to the present. The Talmud often reminds us that we must feel as if certain events, such as the exodus from Egypt, and the receiving of the Law at Mt. Sinai, happened to each of us as well as to our ancestors. For our lives as Jews are greatly influenced by these events.

Now that you have learned something about calendars, especially the Jewish calendar, you will be ready to read about the Jewish holidays which have such an important place on this calendar. In the stories which follow, you will see how an American Jewish family of today celebrates the various holidays of the Jewish year.

THINGS TO DO AND TALK ABOUT
SOMETHING ABOUT CALENDARS

Reviewing the Story

1. In what ways are calendars helpful to us?
2. What causes day and night?
3. What causes the seasons of the year?
4. What three kinds of calendars are there?
5. Give two examples of solar calendars.
6. Give three examples of calendars which have lunar months.
7. Explain the following statement: Although the Jewish calendar is chiefly a *lunar* one, it is also based on the *solar* system.
8. Discuss the different ways in which years used to be numbered among ancient peoples.
9. What three different groups of people contributed to the development of our *everyday* calendar, which is commonly used throughout the world? Tell what each contributed.
10. How was the day of the new moon decided upon by the ancient Hebrews?
11. How was the message spread among the Jews?
12. How did the custom of observing holidays for two days begin?
13. What groups in Jewish life maintain this custom? What groups keep some holidays only one day?

For Classroom Conversation

1. Imagine a world in which there are no calendars. Describe some of the difficulties that would arise in your own life

in such a world. Do you think there would be any advantages? Discuss.

Suggested Activities

Make a Jewish calendar for the year. Get a copy of one for this year and find out when the holidays occur. The Jewish New Year comes on the first day of the *seventh* month, *Tishri.* The *first* month of the calendar year is *Nisan,* which occurs in the spring.

As decoration for your calendar, you might make pictures of ancient peoples and how they planned their first calendars.

ROSH HASHONOH

THE congregation stood in hushed silence as the stirring call of the shofar sounded through the house of worship. It was a solemn moment in the service of Rosh Hashonoh, one of the most holy days of the Jewish year. As the notes died away, the voices of the worshipers rose in prayer.

To Simon Levy, who was sitting in one of the front rows, it was a new experience to be in a synagogue like this. He had arrived in the city just a few days ago, from a small town in the West where there were only a few Jewish families. It was amazing to him that this vast congregation was made up entirely of Jews. In all his eleven years he had never been in such a large and stately synagogue. He was pleasantly excited by the many new things that were happening to him.

After the services, a hub-bub of greetings arose. "Happy New Year! Happy New Year!" flew from lips to lips. A number gave the greeting in Hebrew, according to the old custom. "L'shonoh Tovoh Tikosevu," they said, which means, "May you be inscribed for a good year."

15

Simon walked out with his uncle and aunt, Dr. and Mrs. Jonathon, and his three cousins, thirteen-year-old Maurice, blue-eyed, freckled Ruthie, who was ten, and little five-year-old Naomi. He felt proud to be seen with this charming family. It seemed as if everyone stopped and greeted them. Simon was shy but happy as he was introduced to a number of friends while the slowly moving crowd made its way to the doors. "I want you to meet Simon, my nephew," his Uncle Phil was saying again. "He is going to spend a whole year with us. His parents went to South America and so they loaned him to us."

"How nice that Maury will have a companion," one of them said.

"Me, too," Ruth chimed in. "He's going to be my friend too," and she squeezed his hand warmly.

The September air was brisk, and it was pleasant to walk leisurely home among the well-dressed holiday crowd. "You like it here with us, don't you, Simon?" Ruthie looked up at him with a gay smile that made her eyes and tilted nose crinkle up in a funny, delightful fashion.

"He doesn't like to be bothered with girls all the time, remember that," Maury told her with the superior air that always made her perfectly furious. "And please bear in mind," he added in a tone of freezing dignity, "that you're only a little girl of ten."

"Why—why," Ruthie was about to prove he was right by bursting into angry tears, but Simon squeezed her hand and said shyly, "Ruthie's O.K., Maury." And the rest of the way he kept hold of her hand.

When they reached home, they gathered around the attractive table, set with the best dishes and decorated with flowers in honor of Rosh Hashonoh. Dr. Jonathon recited the holiday Kiddush over the silver goblet of wine. After saying the prayer in Hebrew, he repeated part of it in English. "Blessed art Thou, O Lord our God, King of the Universe, who createst the fruit of the vine. Blessed art Thou, O Lord our God, King of the Universe, who hast kept us in life, and hast taken care of us, and enabled us to reach this season."

Over the two loaves of white bread twists that lay at the head of the table, Dr. Jonathon chanted, "Blessed art Thou, O Lord our God, who bringest forth bread from the earth."

On the table stood a dish of honey surrounded by slices of apple. Each one took a piece of apple, dipped it in the honey and ate it, reciting the Hebrew blessing, "Blessed art Thou, O Lord our God, who createst the fruit of the tree."

"It is an old custom," Uncle Phil explained, "to eat something sweet on Rosh Hashonoh as a symbol for a sweet New Year."

"What's the matter, Simon?" asked Aunt Elsa. "You look a little bewildered."

"I guess I am," the boy admitted. "You see, I'm having so many new experiences here. At home, we didn't celebrate the Jewish holidays very much. There are so few Jewish families in our town, we sort of forgot about most of the holidays. And even on Rosh Hashonoh, we didn't have all these interesting ceremonies. Last night, when the holiday began and you lit candles on the table and everything, it seemed sort of strange. But I liked it very much," he added.

There was little conversation for awhile as all settled down to the pleasant task of enjoying the holiday meal. But Simon continued to look thoughtful as he ate. "Just what do those words *Rosh Hashonoh* mean, Uncle Phil, and what is this holiday all about?"

"I see you won't be taking things for granted, Simon," his uncle smiled at him. "We'll have to be explaining a good many things as we go along. That might be a good idea for the other children too. They are so accustomed to our observance of holidays and ceremonies, they don't ask enough questions. Now about Rosh Hashonoh—the words are Hebrew and mean *Head of the Year*. Rosh Hashonoh and the holiday which comes ten days later, Yom Kippur, are known as the High Holy Days, because they are the most solemn occasions of the Jewish year.

They are different in some other ways, too, from the rest
of the Jewish holidays. You see, most of our festivals are
connected with some important event in the history of the
Jewish people, or with the agricultural life which our ancestors led in Palestine in ancient times. But the High
Holy Days are different. They are occasions for thinking
about our conduct and for repenting of our wrongdoing."

"I always think of Rosh Hashonoh and Yom Kippur in
a little rhyme," Aunt Elsa added. " 'Holy days to consider
our ways.' It seems as if most of the time we are too busy
to think much about these things—how we are behaving
to our family and friends, to the Jewish people, to the
whole world, in fact. But on the High Holy Days we put
everything else aside and spend the time in thought and
prayer. We ask forgiveness for past sins and resolve to lead
better lives in the future."

"I like to hear the blowing of the shofar in the synagogue," Maury said. "It's sort of exciting—like calling
the people to arms or something."

"It is an important part of the Rosh Hashonoh service,"
his father replied. "The shofar is made of a ram's horn,"
he went on, in answer to Simon's inquiring look. "I think
it's a very interesting musical instrument. The Bible men-
tions it many times. As Maury suggested, it was used as a
call to arms, in times of war. But it had many other uses.
The shofar summoned the people together for an assembly

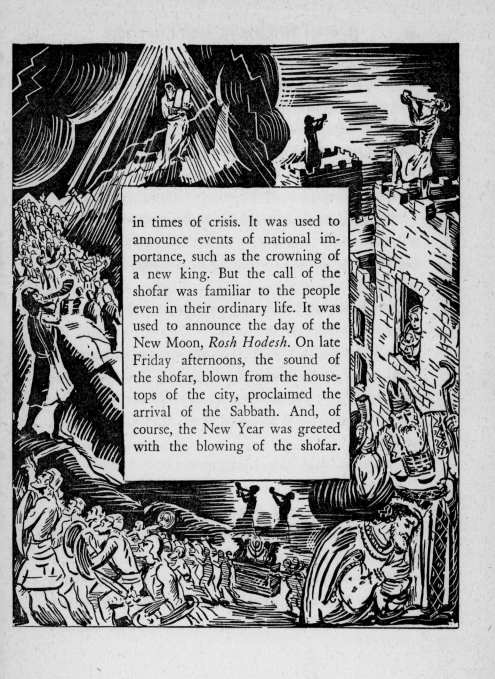

in times of crisis. It was used to announce events of national importance, such as the crowning of a new king. But the call of the shofar was familiar to the people even in their ordinary life. It was used to announce the day of the New Moon, *Rosh Hodesh*. On late Friday afternoons, the sound of the shofar, blown from the housetops of the city, proclaimed the arrival of the Sabbath. And, of course, the New Year was greeted with the blowing of the shofar.

"I guess that's why we heard it today," put in Ruthie.

"The shofar call also makes us think of certain important events in Jewish history," Dr. Jonathon continued, when he saw how interested the children were in this subject. "It reminds us of the thrilling moments at Mt. Sinai when the Israelites received the Ten Commandments while the loud blasts of the trumpet sounded through the desert air. It recalls also the mournful occasion of the destruction of the Temple in Jerusalem—perhaps because the trumpet call was used in battle as a signal to advance or retreat."

"On Rosh Hashonoh, the call of the shofar might be regarded as a call to conscience," Aunt Elsa added. "It says, 'What ho, there! Stop rushing around so much and think more about where you are going. Are you on the right road? Are you making the most of your life?' It is a warning signal to 'Stop, Look, and Listen' to the voice of conscience."

"Very well said," Dr. Jonathon nodded.

But his wife was looking at her youngest daughter. "Naomi, what are you doing?" she cried. "You've eaten every bit of that big dish of honey. I hope it doesn't make you ill."

"It's good," Naomi replied calmly as she daintily wiped her sticky fingers on a napkin. "Now I'll be sure to have a sweet year."

After dinner, the family wandered into the living room. "The High Holy Days always bring me back to the period of my boyhood," Dr. Jonathon remarked as he relaxed in an armchair.

"Tell us about it," Ruthie demanded.

"They were events of the greatest importance in our little village in Lithuania," her father began, always glad to talk of those far-off days. "For a whole month before the holidays arrived, there was an atmosphere of solemn waiting and expectancy. People said their prayers more earnestly and watched their behavior more carefully. In all the little wooden cottages with their thatched roofs, preparations went on for days ahead of time. Floors were freshly scrubbed, the huge tiled stoves were made ready for the winter, the brass samovars where the steaming tea was boiled shone with cleanliness, and the silver candlesticks were polished until they gleamed.

"But far more important than these things was the preparation of one's soul. For it was believed that on Rosh Hashonoh God judges each one and decides his fate for the coming year. On Yom Kippur the decree is made final and the judgment is sealed."

"Tell Simon about the *Three Books*," Maury suggested.

"There is an old belief among Jews," Dr. Jonathon replied, "that on Rosh Hashonoh three books are opened in heaven. In one, the names of those who were completely wicked are inscribed; their fate is death. In another, the names of the righteous are written and sealed for life, while in the third book are put the names of those who were neither very wicked nor very good. For them, judgment is suspended until Yom Kippur. If by that time they have repented, their names are entered in the *Book of Life*. The ten days from Rosh Hashonoh through Yom Kippur are called the *Days of Penitence*.

"Some rabbis have explained this story in the following way. When we do good deeds we feel happy. There is a sort of warm glow around our hearts. We feel a greater joy in being alive. We have really inscribed ourselves in the *Book of Life* by right living, for our bodies are healthier when we are happy. But when we do wrong, sadness and fear creep over us. We worry about what will happen as the result of our bad acts. Often, these feelings actually make us ill. But if we are sorry for our misdeeds and try to correct the wrongs we have done, peace comes into our hearts once more, and new strength and hope. That is the real meaning of the story of the three books."

"Tell us more, daddy," Ruthie begged. "About the time when you were a boy, and Rosh Hashonoh, and everything."

"Well, let me see." He closed his eyes and leaned his head against the chair. "One of the things that stands out

very clearly in my mind when I think of this season of
the year, is the *Selihos* services. Selihos are special prayers
asking forgiveness. They are recited several days before
Rosh Hashonoh, and also between Rosh Hashonoh and
Yom Kippur. Selihos are said in the early hours of the
morning, long before dawn. How well I remember, especially the first Selihos service. When the quiet village
street was still wrapped in sleep, the heavy thump, thump,
thump of footsteps upon the wooden sidewalks would be
heard. It was the sexton from the synagogue. In one hand
he carried a heavy cane and in the other, a large lantern in
which burned the dim, flickering light of a candle. Rap-
ping sharply on the window shutters, he called out in a
deep voice, 'Selihos! Time to arise for Selihos! Arouse
yourself to worship the Creator.'

"I remember with what a feeling of pleasant excitement I dressed hastily in the dark. With a strange, eerie
feeling, I walked beside my father towards the synagogue.
The flickering lanterns cast weird lights on other hurrying, shadowy figures, and footsteps sounded strangely
loud in the quiet of the night. In the synagogue itself, the
swaying figures in the dim light of the candles, the chanting tearful voices reciting the prayers, gave me a thrill of
mystery and strangeness."

"Do people go to Selihos services at the present time?"
Simon asked, much interested.

"Oh, yes," Maury interrupted. "We went to the first Selihos, didn't we, dad? That was before you came, Simon. I liked it. It seemed so strange, going to the synagogue late at night, after twelve o'clock. There was a cantor and a choir and they sang some beautiful hymns."

"There is another special ceremony which you might like to hear about," Dr. Jonathon told them. "It is observed on the afternoon of Rosh Hashonoh by many Jews. This ceremony is called *Tashlich*."

"What is it about?" Ruthie and Simon demanded in the same breath.

"Tashlich," Dr. Jonathon explained, "is a prayer recited on the banks of a river or some other body of fresh water. Flowing water is the symbol of purity and this prayer asks for forgiveness and purification. This ceremony represents man's desire to repent of his wrongdoing and his resolve to start the new year with a clear record."

"Of course," Aunt Elsa put in, "we mustn't think that just going through the ceremony of Tashlich will free us of the responsibility of our acts. It is only a symbol of what should go on within our hearts on Rosh Hashonoh."

"What does the word *Tashlich* mean?" Maury wanted to know.

"It is from a passage in the Bible found in the *Book of Micah*, which is recited during the ceremony. 'And Thou wilt cast all their sins into the depths of the sea.' *Tashlich* is the Hebrew for *Thou wilt cast,*" Dr. Jonathon explained.

"And now," Aunt Elsa suggested, "I think an hour of rest might be a good idea for all of us, if we are going to pay some New Year calls later on."

"An excellent idea, my dear," Uncle Phil agreed.

But Simon had one more question. "How long does Rosh Hashonoh last?" he wanted to know.

"Orthodox and Conservative Jews observe it for two days," his uncle told him. "Reform Jews keep it for one day."

As Simon curled up on the sofa in the living room, he picked up a pile of New Year greeting cards which were lying on a small table. "May I look at these, Aunt Elsa?"

"Of course. We received a good many this year."

"We made some in our class at the Synagogue School," Ruthie told him. "I sent them to my friends."

"Will I go to that school, too, auntie?"

"Surely," she replied. "You want to learn about the other Jewish holidays, don't you?"

"Yes," decided Simon. "I think I do."

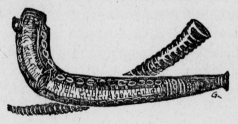

THINGS TO DO AND TALK ABOUT
ROSH HASHONOH

Reviewing the Story

1. Imagine you are Simon, the boy in the story. You are in the synagogue on the morning of Rosh Hashonoh. Now, think out loud and tell what you see, hear, and feel.
2. What ceremonies were performed at the table on the day of Rosh Hashonoh when the Jonathon family returned from the synagogue?
3. On what occasions in ancient times was the shofar regularly used by the Jews?
4. Of what important events in Jewish history does the blowing of the shofar remind us?
5. What reasons do you see for blowing the shofar in the synagogue on Rosh Hashonoh?
6. What is the purpose of the Selihos services? Describe a Selihos service in Eastern Europe.
7. What is the meaning of the Tashlich ceremony? Do you know of any ceremonies in other religions where water is used in connection with the idea of purifying?

For Classroom Conversation

1. Tell in what ways Rosh Hashonoh is celebrated in your home as it is in the story. In what ways isn't it?
2. Why do Jews regard this holiday as a very important one?
3. Do you think there is any value in making New Year resolutions? Discuss. Tell about some resolution which you made in the past and whether you were able to keep it or not.

4. Tell about some other ceremonies besides religious ones in which you have taken part. Did you enjoy them?

Suggested Activities

1.

Making New Year Cards—Use small correspondence cards. Print a New Year greeting on each one, both in English and Hebrew. Decorate the cards. You can use crayon, water-colors, colored pencils, pen and ink, poster paint, or gold gilt paint.

2.

Dramatizing Scenes and Ceremonies—For the next class meeting, be prepared to dramatize a scene or one of the ceremonies described in the story. Work with one or more of your classmates, if necessary. Dress up like the persons in the scene, if you wish to.

3.

Starting a Picture Story Book—Start a picture story book on *Jewish Holidays in Eastern Europe* and show how Uncle Phil in the story observed the holidays and customs when he was a boy. If you like, you can call your book, *When Uncle Phil Was a Boy*.

This might be a class book to which different children would contribute pictures for each holiday. The whole class might draw pictures and the best ones could be selected for the book.

It would be interesting to make your pictures quite large, perhaps several feet long and several feet wide. Use crayons, charcoal, or paint. Make a large cardboard cover for your book and decorate it. Make perforations in the cover so that you can pull cord through and bind your book. You should be able to open it easily each time you add pictures.

4.

Starting an Individual Scrapbook—Start a scrapbook which you will keep throughout the year on *Holiday Ceremonies in the Jewish Home and Synagogue.* Another title for your scrapbook might be, *How We Observe the Jewish Holidays.* Make up your own title if you like.

You can draw pictures for your scrapbook, cut pictures out of magazines, take photographs of ceremonies, write original stories and poems, write descriptions of ceremonies, or follow any other plan which you might think of.

5.

See *Blessings Used Throughout the Story, In English and Hebrew,* beginning on page 226.

YOM KIPPUR

THE eve of Yom Kippur was approaching. Ruthie could see the sun in the western sky as she stopped by the window for a moment, holding two white candles in her hands. She moved slowly to the table and set them in the silver candlesticks. Everything was ready for the meal which would soon be eaten in preparation for the fast. After that, it was forbidden to eat or drink until the end of the following day, except for children under thirteen years of age, or for those who were ill.

"Mother, how much time is there before the blessing of the candles?" Ruthie asked, stepping to the door leading to the kitchen, where Mrs. Jonathon was still busy.

"About fifteen minutes, dear. Is there something else you should do?"

"Well, I'm not exactly sure." Ruthie spoke in a low, hesitating voice. "You know what daddy told us last night about making peace with everyone before Yom Kippur.

He said that before we ask God to forgive us, we should seek forgiveness of our fellow-men."

"Yes, dear, that's right," her mother agreed quietly.

"Well, Judy and I haven't spoken to each other for two whole days. That's a long time, considering she's my best friend. But she was really wrong, mother, and she should speak to me first."

"Pride is one of the things for which we shall ask forgiveness in the synagogue tomorrow," Mrs. Jonathon remarked as she carefully lifted a fragrant brown honey cake from the oven. "You'll have to decide quickly what you are going to do about it, dear. The time is very short."

Ruthie walked slowly away, a troubled expression on her face. Then suddenly she hurried out of the house to the next building where Judy lived. A pleased look came into Mrs. Jonathon's face, and it wasn't because of the excellent cake she was looking at.

Soon the family was gathered around the table. There was a contented look in Ruth's face that showed she was at peace with the world—and with Judy.

Before they started for the synagogue, Dr. Jonathon called each member of the family to him for a blessing, just as he did on the eve of the Sabbath. The family walked to the synagogue in a quiet and thoughtful mood.

Every seat was taken, for Yom Kippur brought to the house of worship many of those who did not attend synagogue services regularly. The services began with the beautiful chant of *Kol Nidre*. As the cantor and choir began the opening strains, the large congregation listened in almost breathless silence. The festival of the Great White Fast had begun.

After the services, the Jonathons spent the rest of the evening quietly at home. The holiday candles on the table were burning low. Simon asked about another light that had been lit. It was in a small glass filled with tallow.

"That is a memorial light, which we burn on Yom Kippur in memory of those who have passed away," Aunt Elsa told him. "It is generally called a *Yiskor* light, after the first word of the Hebrew prayer recited in their memory."

"Well, Simon, I can see another question in your eyes," his uncle smiled at him encouragingly. "Go ahead and ask it."

"It's such a simple one, I hesitate to ask it," the boy admitted. "But I would like to know why people fast on Yom Kippur."

"Fasting is a way of showing our repentance for the wrongs we have done. It puts us into a more humble frame of mind as we pray for forgiveness. The words *Yom Kippur,* you know, mean *Day of Atonement.* By fasting, we show that we want to atone, or make up, for our wrongdoing. We also prove that on this day we can resist the temptations of the body and turn our minds and hearts entirely to the duty of thinking about our conduct and seeking forgiveness."

"We've been studying some of the Yom Kippur prayers in religious school," Maury said. "Why will everybody recite such a long confession of sins during the services tomorrow? I'm sure very few people could be guilty of all those wicked things."

"You're quite right," his father replied. "I doubt whether even one person in our congregation tomorrow will be guilty of all those wrongdoings contained in the prayer, *I Confess.* But when we Jews pray, it must be not only for ourselves, but for all Israel. When we ask forgiveness, it is not only for our own wrongdoing, but for the sins of others. For we do not know in what ways our behavior might have caused another person to do wrong.

Furthermore, the fate of all Israel is bound together. It is an old Jewish motto that 'all Jews are responsible for one another.' "

"This is a good time for a nice Yom Kippur story, daddy," Ruthie coaxed, sitting down on the arm of his chair. "With the candles burning low, and everything sort of quiet, it puts me in the mood for stories."

"You're always in the mood for stories," he reminded her. "Well, let's see." He thought for a moment. "I'll tell you one I've always liked. My father used to tell it to me on Yom Kippur.

"Once upon a time, there was an angel who disobeyed God. The angel was summoned to appear before the Throne of Judgment to answer for his misdeed. He pleaded for mercy and begged God to forgive him. God looked down upon the angel kindly and said, 'I shall not punish you, but you must atone for your wrongdoing. I will give you a task to perform. Go down to earth and bring to Me the most precious thing in the world.'

"The angel sped down to earth, happy to have a chance to win God's forgiveness. Over many countries he roamed, for many years, looking for the most precious thing in the world. One day, he came upon a great battlefield. He saw a young soldier lying there, badly wounded. This young man had fought bravely in the defense of his country, and was now dying. The angel caught up the last drop of blood from the soldier's wound and hastened back to heaven with it.

" 'This is indeed a precious thing which you have brought back,' God said to the angel. 'A soldier who gives his life for his country is very dear to Me. But return, and search once more.'

"So the angel returned to earth and continued his quest. For many years he roamed, through cities, woods, and plains. Then, one day, he saw a nurse in a great hospital. She was dying of a dread disease. She had nursed others through this disease, working so hard that she had worn down her own strength and so caught the illness herself. She lay pale and gasping upon her cot. As she was dying, the angel caught up her last breath and hastened to heaven with it.

" 'Surely, God,' said the angel, 'the last breath of this unselfish nurse is the most precious thing in the world.'

" 'It is a very precious thing that you have brought to Me,' God replied. 'One who gives his life for another is indeed worthy in My sight. But return, and search again.'

"Then the angel returned to earth again to search once more. Far and wide he roamed, for many years. One night, he saw a villainous-looking man on horseback, riding through a dark forest. The man was armed with a sword and a spear. The angel guessed on what wicked errand this man was bound. He was going to avenge himself on the keeper of the forest, who would not permit him to poach on the king's game. The man came to the small hut where the forester and his family lived. Light streamed from the window. Getting down from his horse, the villain peered through the window. He saw the wife of the forester putting her little son to bed. He heard her teaching him how to say his evening prayers. Something within his hard heart seemed to melt. Did the scene bring back memories of his own far-away childhood and his own mother, who had also taught him to pray? Tears filled the man's eyes and he turned away from his evil deed and repented of his ways. The angel caught up one of his tears and flew back to heaven with it.

" 'This,' said God, 'is the most precious thing in the world, for it is the tear of a repentant sinner. And repentance opens the gates of Heaven.' "

There was a moment of silence as Uncle Phil finished. He smiled at the children's interested faces. "Well, I guess that's all, children. It might be a good idea to go to bed early tonight."

"Are you going to fast all day, today?" Ruthie asked Simon the next morning.

"Yes, all day," he answered firmly.

"You don't have to," Maury put in. "You're not thirteen yet, like I am."

"Well," Simon insisted, "I have to get into practice. Anyhow, it isn't very hard to fast."

"Oh, no?" Maury smiled loftily at the younger boy. "That's what you think when you're only eleven and don't really *have* to. But just wait a few hours and we'll see."

"We will indeed," Simon replied with dignity, while Ruthie giggled.

During the morning, Simon followed the services with much interest. "All over the world," his uncle had told him on the way to the synagogue, "Jews will gather in synagogues and temples to observe the Day of Atonement."

"Even in China and Australia?" Ruthie asked.

"Everywhere," her father replied. "In the distant lands of Persia and Iraq, in the freezing steppes of Siberia and the tropical lands of the equator, Jews will meet in their houses of worship for an entire day of prayer and fasting." Simon was thinking of this as he looked over the large congregation bowed in prayer.

After the sermon, about one o'clock, Simon and the Jonathon children went home for a rest. "Come back in the late afternoon for the concluding services," Dr. Jonathon told them.

Mrs. Jonathon, who had a slight headache, went home with them, to rest for a little while.

"Are you still fasting, Simon?" Ruthie whispered, her blue eyes dancing.

"Are you still fasting, Simon?" Naomi echoed in her usual fashion, even imitating the tones of her big sister's voice. The boy nodded, trying not to look too well-pleased.

"Oh, you must be awfully hungry by this time." There was a teasing admiration in Ruth's tone. "How could you resist those delicious cinnamon buns that Naomi and I had for breakfast! And we're going to have roast chicken for lunch." Her eyes twinkled mischievously as Simon glared at her. But one couldn't lose one's temper right after a Yom Kippur service.

How the thought of that roast chicken tempted his empty stomach! Never in all his life had he been so hungry, Simon decided. After all, he was only eleven and didn't have to fast all day. Then he remembered how he had loftily assured Maury that he would. Simon's pale lips took on a more determined line. He would stick to his resolution.

Shortly after they reached home, Mrs. Jonathon called out, "Lunch is ready, Simon."

"No, thank you, Aunt Elsa, I'm still fasting," he said politely.

"But I don't think you should fast all day," she replied gently. "This is your first experience and it's after one o'clock now."

"Oh, it doesn't bother me." He tried to make his voice sound indifferent.

"Just why do you want to fast all day?" his aunt asked, looking at him seriously. "Is it for the reasons we were discussing last night—the worthwhile reasons for fasting—or is it a matter of pride?"

"He wants to show me he can do it," Maury put in unkindly. Simon flushed deeply, but he had the rare quality of being completely honest with himself.

"I guess you're right, Aunt Elsa," he admitted. "I—I'll have lunch, if I may."

Maury was taken by surprise at this turn of events. Then he burst out, "Gee, Simon, I think you're swell. To admit that took more courage than fasting would have." At these words, Simon's face brightened wonderfully. Aunt Elsa looked proudly at both her boys, and Ruthie was through with her teasing.

Late in the afternoon, Simon, Maury, and Ruth entered the synagogue and took their places. Soon the *N'iloh,* or concluding service, began. A stir of new interest seemed to sweep over the congregation. The cantor's voice took on a deeper note. The choir sang with greater feeling. Soon the Day of Atonement would be at an end. What did the coming year hold for each of these worshipers? Earnestly the rabbi prayed, "The day is fading, the sun is setting; the silence and peace of night descend upon the earth.

Grant rest, O God, unto our disquieted hearts; lift up the soul that is cast down. Turn, in Thine all-forgiving love, to Thy children who yearn for Thy mercy. Let this hour bring the assurance that Thou hast forgiven—" the earnest voice went on.

As the dusk began to fall, the notes of the shofar rose triumphantly on the air. The people of Israel had made their peace with God. With light hearts and merry greetings, the congregation moved slowly out, the rabbi's benediction upon them. "The Lord bless thy going out and thy coming in, from this time forth, even for ever. Amen."

THINGS TO DO AND TALK ABOUT
YOM KIPPUR

Reviewing the Story

1. Describe the activities that take place in the Jonathon home before the family leaves for the synagogue on the eve of Yom Kippur.
2. What reasons are given for fasting on Yom Kippur?
3. Why do the prayers on Yom Kippur contain confessions of many more kinds of sins than any one person would be guilty of?
4. Why was the story told by Uncle Phil a good Yom Kippur story?
5. Why did Simon want to fast and what made him change his mind?

For Classroom Conversation

1. Does Yom Kippur have any meaning for children, or is it just for grown-ups?
2. Give some examples to show that wrongdoing often brings its own punishment.
3. Do you think that wrongdoing ever brings a lasting reward? Discuss this honestly and freely.
4. Do you admire Ruthie for speaking to Judy first, on Yom Kippur eve? Is pride always a fault? Give examples of a good kind of pride and an undesirable kind of pride.
5. Why was Aunt Elsa proud of both Simon and Maury at the end of the story?
6. Find out, if you can, what part fasting has in other religions.

Suggested Activities

1.

Read aloud parts of the dialogue in the story, different children impersonating different characters.

2.

Write a letter to yourself telling what faults you will try to overcome during the coming year. Below the letter, write the twelve months of the year. Put the letter away in a safe place. Take it out on the first day of each month and read it over. Check yourself to see if you are keeping up your resolutions.

3.

Make up a prayer of your own that you think would be suitable for a children's service on Yom Kippur. Read it at the next meeting of the class.

4.

Draw a large picture illustrating some scene in the story.

5.

Make up a story like the one Uncle Phil tells the children, putting in three *different* things which the angel brought back. The story should show *your* idea of what is the most precious thing in the world.

SUKKOS

SIMON was holding a bright-colored gourd in his hand, trying to decide just where to hang it. He looked thoughtfully all around the large synagogue sukkah, which he and his classmates at religious school were decorating. Simon felt very lucky because his group had been chosen for this pleasant task while other classes were busy with their regular lessons. The sukkah looked lovely, he thought. The walls were covered with the green branches of trees and trailing vines. Against this background were hung fruits of many kinds and colors, and other products of the harvest season. Large, rosy apples, ruddy pears, and clusters of luscious dark grapes hung by their stems on the walls and from the roof. A small bunch of bananas made a splash of golden color near the pale green of quinces. From the roof, which was made of fragrant pine branches, hung festoons of strung popped corn, a vivid white against the green. On the floor, in a corner, stood an autumn sheaf of corn-stalks, and right beside it lay a large, bright-colored pumpkin.

45

Green and red peppers, also strung on cord, made a gay arc across one of the walls.

Simon looked around critically but with a pleasant feeling of accomplishment. His classmates were still dashing about here and there, putting on the finishing touches. He wondered where he should hang the large, gaily-colored gourd which he still held in his hand. He had to find just the right place for this final bit of decoration. Then he spied a bare spot on the roof, at the front of the sukkah. The very place, he decided, for everyone would see it there. He dashed for the ladder, climbed up, and tied on the gourd. His teacher, a pleasant young man of about twenty-two, stood watchfully at the foot of the ladder. He breathed more easily when the boy came down.

And now it was time for the whole school to gather in the sukkah, for the general assembly was to be held there.

The admiring exclamations of the children who came flocking in at the sound of the bell was sweet praise to those who had done the task. Simon looked up at his own special gourd and gave it a friendly smile.

The assembly service began with a song of thanksgiving for the bountiful harvest season. In the fragrant and colorful atmosphere of the sukkah, even the city children felt the breath of fields and orchards and the richness of the fertile earth. As the rabbi began to talk about the significance of this festival, Simon listened intently. This was

the first real Sukkos of his experience and he found it tremendously interesting.

"Many, many centuries ago," the rabbi was saying, "our ancestors lived as farmers in the land of Canaan. Long before America was discovered, centuries before Christianity was founded, the ancient Hebrews were plowing the soil of Palestine and planting seed. They lived in small villages, in huts of sun-baked clay. Their most joyous holiday of the year was the Festival of the Ingathering, when the harvest was completed and the people gave thanks to God for His goodness. That was Sukkos in ancient days, the festival which we still celebrate today.

"As we look about this beautiful booth, we ask ourselves what it means, and why the Jewish people have followed the interesting custom of the sukkah for hundreds of years. The commandment to build the sukkah is given in the Bible, which says, 'The Lord had commanded by Moses that the children of Israel should dwell in booths in the feast of the seventh month; and that they should proclaim in all their cities and in Jerusalem, saying, "Go forth unto the mount and fetch branches of wild olive, and myrtle branches, and palm branches, and branches of thick trees, to make booths, as it is written." So the people went forth and brought them and made themselves booths, every one upon the roof of his house, and in their courts, and in the courts of the house of God, and in the broad place of the

water-gate and in the broad place of the gate of Ephraim.
—And there was great gladness.—And they kept the feast
seven days, and the eighth day was a solemn assembly, according unto the law.'

"A number of reasons have been given to explain this
custom of the sukkah. The Bible tells us that the sukkah
reminds us of the days when our ancestors lived as nomads
in the desert, wandering about from place to place, and
dwelling in tents. The sukkah also serves as a reminder of
the small booths which the farmers of Palestine would
often erect in their fields and vineyards during the harvest
season. There they would sleep, guarding their crops from
thieves and wild animals. We can imagine them lying on
their mats within their loosely-built booths made of the
branches of trees. Through the boughs fell the bright rays
of the brilliant Palestine moon, just as in this sukkah, the
sun is dropping its golden shafts at this moment.

"Other explanations have been added by Jewish scholars
and teachers concerning the meaning of the sukkah. Some
say that it is a symbol of our faith in God, for even though
we leave our sturdy homes and dwell in these frail booths,
we feel confident that God will protect us, just as He did
our ancestors who wandered in the wilderness and lived
in tents. The sukkah may also be a symbol of the insecure
lives which the Jewish people have led during the past two
thousand years, as they wandered from land to land, seek-

ing a safe place in which to live. And yet, throughout their hardships, the Jews have survived. Thus, the sukkah reminds us of our own weakness and of the goodness of God,

who protects us. But, chiefly, it recalls the happy harvest season in Palestine."

After the rabbi was through speaking, a group of children came to the front of the sukkah. They were each carrying a green, slender palm branch, known as a *lulov* in Hebrew, and a fragrant, yellow citron, called an *esrog*. Each palm branch had some small branches of a willow tree fastened to it on one side, and some myrtle branches on the other side. These four kinds of plants are used at Sukkos to represent the fruitfulness of the earth at this harvest season. Orthodox Jews recite a blessing over them every morning of the Sukkos festival.

The children displayed their plants. They sang songs and recited poems about them. Within that colorful sukkah, everyone felt the presence of the happy harvest season.

After the assembly, Simon and the Jonathon children walked home together, talking about the sukkah and the interesting things the rabbi had told them. Mrs. Jonathon met them at the door. "I have a surprise for you," she cried. "We've all been invited to spend the second part of the Sukkos festival with Aunt Bess and Uncle David. You know, Simon, they haven't seen much of you since your arrival, and they're eager to have you. Grandfather lives with them and he is looking forward to your visit."

"I'll bet Cousin Danny is too," put in Ruthie excitedly. "Oh, mother, I'm so glad Maury and I are going too."

"I'm so glad I'm going too," echoed Naomi, beginning to hop around the room on one foot, as she usually did when excited.

"I think Sukkos is a grand holiday," Simon declared. "I like the way it's divided into two parts, with half holidays in between."

On the afternoon of the seventh day of Sukkos, several hours before sunset, the Jonathon family and Simon started on the trip for the distant suburb where their relatives lived. "We want to get there before evening," Dr. Jonathon said, "or grandfather will have left for the synagogue. You know, tonight is Yom Tov."

"Aunt Bess and Uncle David are very Orthodox," Maury informed Simon. "That's one reason why grandfather lives with them."

"They have a sukkah all their own," Ruthie chimed in eagerly. "It's in their backyard. And we'll eat our meals there and everything."

Dr. Jonathon stopped his car in front of a simple two-family brick house. Twelve-year-old Danny, who was waiting for them on the porch, gave a whoop of delight. Aunt Bess, glowing with welcome, hurried to the door and gave each child a big hug and a kiss in her warm-hearted fashion. "It's so good to see you all," she cried. "Come in. Here is grandfather. He's been talking of nothing but you children all day. I think he's been even more impatient for your coming than Danny."

"Of course I was," grandfather smiled as he embraced them. "And look at them—why shouldn't I be proud to be their grandfather!"

The men and boys now had to hurry off to the synagogue. Ruthie and Aunt Elsa helped to set the table in the

sukkah for the evening meal. "It's beautiful," Ruthie cried
as she stopped with a pile of plates in her hands and looked
around admiringly. The green-covered walls of the sukkah were generously decorated with fruits and flowers of
all kinds and colors. Through the green branches of the
roof glinted the warm rays of the setting sun. The air was
fragrant with a mingling of delightful odors—the smell
of fresh flowers and pine branches. The table looked very
nice, Ruthie thought, with its shining white cloth, spar-
kling silver, and dainty-stemmed glassware. The candles,
which had just been lit, glowed in the silver candlesticks.
At the head of the table lay two long twists of golden
white bread, covered with an embroidered cloth. Nearby
stood a goblet for wine and a filled decanter. Ruthie ar-
ranged the dinner plates, handling them very carefully
for they were her aunt's best dishes. Now Aunt Bess came
in to say the blessing over the candles. Ruth enjoyed the
lovely scene. Aunt Bess spread her hands over the lights
and then covered her face as she said the following prayer
in Hebrew. "Blessed art Thou, O Lord our God, King of
the Universe, who hast sanctified us by thy commandments, and commanded us to light the festival lights."

Very soon the front door was flung open and the sound
of merry voices filled the air. "Good Yom Tov, Good Yom
Tov," everyone cried.

They gathered around the table and remained standing

while grandfather filled the goblet with wine and chanted the Kiddush in a beautiful melody. Then came the ritual washing of the hands, which is customary before every meal by Orthodox Jews. Simon did as the others, pouring a glass of water first over one hand and then over the other. As he dried them on a towel, he repeated the Hebrew prayer after his grandfather. "Blessed art Thou, O Lord, our God, King of the Universe, who hast sanctified us by thy commandments and commanded us concerning the washing of the hands."

When they were all seated at the table, grandfather repeated a prayer over the bread. "Blessed art Thou, O Lord, our God, King of the Universe, who hast brought forth bread from the earth." Each one repeated the prayer and ate a piece of the bread which was passed around.

Then came one of Aunt Bess's delicious holiday dinners.

After grace was said, the children followed grandfather into the living room and gathered around his chair. "This is one time when you get a vacation, Phil," smiled his wife. "It looks like grandfather will be doing the talking tonight."

"Perhaps I shouldn't admit it, Elsa, but I think I shall miss being the center of their attention. It's rather fun, you know."

Simon promptly spied a lulov and esrog, which were standing on a table. He picked them up and examined them. "The willow branches are a bit faded, grandfather," he said critically, "and the twigs of myrtle are losing some of their leaves. But your esrog is very nice, and so is the lulov."

"Well, you seem to be quite an expert on the subject," grandfather replied, with a twinkle in his eye. "But this happens to be the seventh day of Sukkos. The blessing over these four species is recited only on the mornings of the first seven days of the festival so these plants have already served their purpose."

"You see, little boys shouldn't be so clever," Maury put in teasingly.

"Come, I'll show you just how it is done," grandfather suggested. "The esrog is held in the left hand and the lulov in the right. The following blessing is recited, 'Blessed art Thou, O Lord our God, King of the Universe, who has sanctified us by thy commandments and commanded us to take the lulov.' "

"Does everybody here say it too?" asked Naomi.

"Every member of the family," her grandfather replied.

"All sorts of interesting meanings have been given to these four species of plants," the old man went on. "You see, the esrog has both beauty and fragrance. The lulov has beauty but no fragrance. The myrtle has fragrance but no beauty, and the willow has neither. They have been compared to four types of people. The esrog stands for the

person who has both beauty and strength of character. The palm branch represents one who has beauty but no strength of character. The myrtle—"

"Stands for strength of character but no beauty," interrupted Simon.

"And the willow for the one who has neither," chanted Ruthie.

"They are also compared to four kinds of Jews," went on their grandfather, who was enjoying himself thoroughly. "The esrog stands for the Jew who is educated in the Torah and does kind deeds. The lulov is the symbol of the Jew who knows Torah but does not practice acts of kindness."

"The myrtle," Simon took up the story, "I suppose, stands for the Jew who is ignorant of the Torah but does kind deeds."

"And the poor willow," Ruthie chanted again, "is both ignorant and unkind. I'm beginning to feel sorry for the willow."

"Talking about the willow makes me think of the services in the synagogue this morning," Danny remarked. "The willow really did get special attention then. The whole congregation formed a procession," he explained to the others, "and we marched around the pews. The rabbi stood on the little platform in the center, holding a scroll of the Torah. Then we all took the willow branches and beat them on the ground until the leaves came off. It was fun."

"Why did they do that, grandfather?" asked Simon.

"Today was the seventh day of the Sukkos festival," the old man replied. It has a special name, all its own—*Hoshano Rabbo*. The prayers which are chanted during this procession that Danny described begin and end with the word *Hoshano,* which means *save us.* Every day of Sukkos, the congregation forms a procession and marches around one time, but on Hoshano Rabbo, the day of the *Great Hoshano,* the procession marches around seven times.

"These ceremonies have remained with us since the days of the Temple in Jerusalem several thousand years ago," grandfather went on. "Sukkos was celebrated with great festivities in those days. There, everyone marched around the great altar, but today we circle around the Torah in the synagogue, for the Torah is now the center of Jewish life."

"You haven't explained why they beat the willow branches on the ground, the way Danny said they did," Simon reminded him.

"That custom, too, has survived from Temple days," grandfather explained. "It is a symbolic way of asking for a fertile crop. The willow grows on the banks of streams and in other moist places and therefore represents plentiful rain and a good soil."

For the rest of the evening, grandfather told them more about Sukkos. Simon learned that this festival is the longest of the Jewish year. It consists of nine days. After the first two days come five half-holidays. The seven days of Sukkos are followed by *Sh'mini Atseres,* the Eighth Day of Solemn Assembly. It is no longer really necessary to eat in the sukkah after the seventh day, but many people like to do so. The ninth day of the holiday is *Simhas Torah,* Rejoicing in the Law. On this day, the reading of the Torah, which has taken a whole year, is concluded, and then immediately begun again. A portion of the Torah is read in the synagogue every Sabbath. Simhas Torah expresses the joy of the Jewish people in their precious possession, the Torah.

The next two days which the children spent with their relatives were very happy ones. Simon especially enjoyed the services in the synagogue on Simhas Torah. On this occasion, even the women and girls, who usually sit up in the gallery in the Orthodox synagogue, may come into the main hall of worship. Simon watched with interest as the scrolls of the Torah were taken out of the Ark. Each scroll was handed to a member of the congregation. A procession was formed, the men bearing the scrolls going first, the children following gaily after them. Some of the boys and girls carried small flags of white and blue. The group circled around the pews, chanting psalms in joyous voices.

A cantor and a choir of young boys led the prayers. Many of those who were seated, reached over and kissed the velvet coverings of the scrolls. Seven times the procession moved around the hall, carrying its precious burden. Thus Israel expressed its joy for the sacred heritage of the Torah which the Jews have given to the world.

It was Simon's first real Simhas Torah, and he found it a very interesting experience.

THINGS TO DO AND TALK ABOUT

SUKKOS

Reviewing the Story

1. What period in Jewish history does Sukkos, the harvest festival, bring to our minds?
2. Read the passage quoted from the Bible which gives the commandment about building a sukkah.
3. Where did the Jews of ancient times build their sukkahs? What material did they use? How long did they observe the festival?
4. Why does the sukkah remind us of the times when our ancestors lived as nomads?
5. Why does the sukkah remind us, also, of the times when the ancient Hebrews were farmers in Palestine?
6. What other meanings does the sukkah have?
7. Describe the sukkah in grandfather's house as Ruthie sees it, just before the holiday meal is served. Tell how the table is set.
8. What prayers are recited by different members of the family, before, during, and after the meal? Make a list of these.
9. What four plants are used in the Sukkos ceremony? Describe this ceremony and tell its meaning.
10. Describe these four plants. To what four types of Jews are they compared?
11. What is the seventh day of the festival called? How is it celebrated in the synagogue?
12. What is the eighth day called?
13. What is the ninth day of the festival? Describe the celebration in the synagogue on this day.

Suggested Activities

Giving a Sukkos Party—If there is a synagogue sukkah, the class party might be held there on some afternoon during the period of the festival. Perhaps some child in the group has a sukkah in his home and would allow the class to decorate the sukkah and have the party there. Another possibility is to have the class undertake the building of a sukkah, either on the grounds of the synagogue or in some child's home. Get some of the fathers of the class to help you.

If none of the above suggestions can be carried out, you might transform your classroom into a sukkah. Cover the walls with green crepe paper and pin or paste decorations on them. These can include branches of trees, fruits, and flowers, made of paper and colored. You can also use real plants, fruits, and flowers. The description of the sukkah in the story should help you.

Another suggestion is to make a miniature sukkah. This can be built of cardboard boxes and wrapping paper.

Added Decorations for the Party—*A Sand Table Scene*—On one half of the sand table show a harvest scene in ancient Palestine, and on the other side, a harvest scene in modern Palestine. For ancient Palestine, show a vineyard, a tower for guarding the crops, and a booth in which the farmer and his family slept during the harvest season. Show people working in the vineyard, dressed in the simple tunic and sash worn by the farmers in biblical days. In one corner of the scene, show a wine press and people pressing the grapes with their feet.[1]

For the harvest scene in modern Palestine, show a Jewish

[1] Note to Teacher: For illustrations of the objects in this scene, see *Pupil's Activity Book*, Volume One, by Dorothy F. Zeligs.

agricultural settlement (kvutza) in the distance, and people working in the fields. They might be harvesting grain with a modern harvesting machine.

The buildings in both scenes could be made of brown corrugated paper having two smooth sides, with the corrugated part between. First, cut out a pattern. Then trace the pattern on the corrugated paper. With a sharp knife, cut along the lines. Wherever you want to bend the paper, cut through one side of the smooth surface only. You can use mending tape to fasten the sides of the building together. Color with poster paint.

The figures can be cut out of cardboard and colored, or made of clay.

Suggestions for the Program—Making a Walt Disney Movie— It would be fun to make an animated movie about the *Four Species,* to show at your party. The following story is suggested for the movie, but you may change it if you like, or make up another story entirely.

*The Story—*The esrog and the lulov have a quarrel because each thinks he is the most important of the four species. The lulov turns pale with rage and begins to dry up. Brown spots of anger appear upon the beautiful esrog. The gentle myrtle tremble with fear at the loud tones of the quarrel and shed their leaves like tears. The poor willow branches droop lower and lower, and finally creep fearfully away and run to the banks of a stream, where they hide under the tree from which they were cut. The lulov and the esrog look about them. They see the poor myrtle with most of their leaves lying on the ground, while the willow branches have disappeared altogether. The lulov and the esrog feel unhappy and ashamed. They realize that without their other two partners, they have lost their own value, for the blessing over the four species cannot be recited without all four. They see, too, that they have lost their beauty because of their anger. They beg each other's forgiveness and wonder how they can repair the damage that has been done. They remind each other that their task was to help the Spirit of Sukkos by recalling to the Jewish people the bounty of the harvest and the goodness of God, who created all species. They appeal to the Spirit of Sukkos for help. She responds and restores their beauty to them. The leaves fly back to the myrtle, and the little willow branches are coaxed out of their hiding place. The story ends with a scene in which a child holds the four species and recites the blessing over them, while the Spirit of Sukkos hovers in the background.

Directions for Making the Movie—The figures can be made of colored paper, cut out, and pasted on a roll of white paper. Of course, the characters should be given faces, hands, and feet, like the characters in a Disney movie.

Each child might be given one scene of the story to prepare. If preferred, each child can work on a separate piece of the film paper, and these panels can later be pasted together. The pictures can be separated from each other by a thin strip of colored paper, if desired.

Use a wooden box with two rollers for showing your movie. The rollers are placed at each end of the open side of the box. They are fastened into holes made in the top and bottom of the box. The rollers should have handles and should be removable. Fasten the film to the rollers and show the movie by turning it from one roller to the other.

If you haven't time to make the wooden box and the rollers, you can just roll the movie on two sticks. Two children can hold it, rolling it from one stick to the other, as needed.

Several children can take part in the explanation of the story as the film is unrolled. It would be more interesting if four children took the part of the four characters and spoke just as in a real, animated movie.

Original Stories and Poems—Plan to read original stories and poems at your party. The following subjects are suggested for stories:

1. How we celebrate Sukkos in our home
2. How grandfather celebrated Sukkos when he was a boy
3. The old rabbi and the esrog—the story of a poor old rabbi who longed for an esrog and how his wish was granted.
4. The disappearance of the esrog—a mystery story

Add other subjects of your own.

Sukkos Songs—Make up your own songs, if you have time. You might choose some familiar tunes and make up words to fit them. Learn some Sukkos songs. The following are suggested:

The Esrog and the Lulov, from *The Gateway to Jewish Song,* by Judith Eisenstein, page 71.

Harvest, from the same book, page 73.

The Garland Song, from *Songs of My People,* by Coopersmith.

Writing the Invitations—If you are inviting your parents or other guests, you might want to send them invitations. Print the invitations on small cards and decorate them with Sukkos symbols.

Planning the Program—Plan the order of the program for the party. Decide what songs, stories, and poems you will have, in addition to the movie film. Decide what refreshments you will serve and just how you will serve them.

Note—If you haven't time for a Sukkos party, you might carry out some of the suggested activities anyhow.

THE SABBATH

SIMON stared sadly through the window at the gray November skies. His school books lay in a rather untidy heap on the maple desk in a corner of his room. The boy suddenly felt lonely and unhappy. He wondered what his mother and father were doing in far-off Rio de Janeiro. If only he could see them for a little while!

It was unusual for Simon to feel that way. He had become so much a part of the Jonathon family, with whom he was spending the year, that he often unthinkingly called his Aunt Elsa *mother* and his Uncle Phil *father,* and then laughed at his error. But it seemed to him that he had hardly seen his relatives all week. Everyone had been so busy that the family had not spent even one evening together. Even now, his cousin Maurice was in the darkened storeroom at one end of the apartment, busy with his favorite hobby, photography. Ruth was taking a piano lesson, and Naomi was out in the park.

Simon thought of the pleasant holidays which they had

all enjoyed together during the past two months—Rosh
Hashonoh, Yom Kippur, Sukkos, and Simhas Torah. But
there were no Jewish holidays in November, the boy real-
ized with a feeling of disappointment. Thanksgiving Day
would help make up for that, but the great American
festival came at the very end of the month, so was still a
long way off. What a dull world it was without holidays!

A sudden gust of wind blew the door of his room open.
A fragrant odor drifted in from the kitchen. Simon sniffed
it curiously. In a moment his gloom vanished. He had forgotten that it was Friday. Only on that day did the kitchen
have those special, delightful odors of cooking. Tonight
everyone would be home. It was family night. There
would be a special Sabbath dinner. He loved Friday nights
and Saturdays.

A banging of doors announced Ruthie's arrival from the
studio. "Si-mon, Si-mon," she called in her sweet, shrill
voice. "Please help me arrange these flowers," she begged
when he appeared. "You always select the right vases and
fix the flowers so that they look just right."

"Flatterer," he laughed. "Just another Tom Sawyer
white-washing the fence." But he went to work gladly
for he loved to arrange the flowers which Aunt Elsa
bought each week for the Sabbath table.

The short November twilight was approaching. Uncle
Phil, home early from his office, was adjusting his tie on a

fresh shirt. He looked ruddy and fresh from his shower. "Sorry I couldn't get home in time for synagogue services this afternoon," he told his wife.

"The eight o'clock evening services will be starting soon," she replied comfortingly. "Then we will be able to go regularly."

Everyone watched as Aunt Elsa lighted the Sabbath candles and recited the blessing over them, first in Hebrew, then in English. She spread her hands over the lights and then held her hands before her face as she prayed, "Blessed art Thou, O Lord our God, King of the Universe, who hast sanctified us by thy commandments and commanded us to kindle the Sabbath lights." Now the Sabbath had officially begun. Dr. Jonathon chanted the popular melody for greeting the Sabbath, and the others joined him.

> "Come, my friend, to meet the bride,
> Let us welcome the Sabbath day."

Simon felt proud because he knew the song in Hebrew, too, by this time. Dr. Jonathon looked affectionately at his wife, and in accordance with the old Jewish custom recited from the *Book of Proverbs* in the Bible,

> "A woman of worth who can find?
> For her price is far above rubies.
> She looketh well to the ways of her household,

And eateth not the bread of idleness.
Her children rise up and call her blessed;
Her husband also, and he praiseth her:
'Many daughters have done valiantly,
But thou excellest them all.'
Grace is deceitful and beauty is vain,
But a woman that feareth the Lord, she shall be
    praised."

Dr. Jonathon then called each one of the children to him
for the Sabbath eve blessing. When his turn came, Simon
stood very still. His uncle placed his hands on the boy's
head and prayed, "God make thee as Ephraim and Manasseh. May the Lord bless thee and keep thee. The Lord
make His face to shine upon thee and be gracious unto
thee. The Lord turn His face unto thee and give thee
peace. Amen."

When he blessed the girls and Aunt Elsa, Dr. Jonathon
began with the words, "God make thee like Sarah and
Rebecca, Rachel and Leah."

Simon's heart was light as everyone sat down at the
table. On the white linen cloth the silverware shone and
the glasses sparkled. The candles in their silver candlesticks gleamed brightly. The autumn flowers in the center
were brilliant with color. Two white loaves of bread were
set at the head of the table.

Dr. Jonathon filled a large silver goblet with wine and pronounced the Kiddush.

"The Sabbath is almost as good as a holiday," Simon declared.

"I think it's better," Ruth declared, "because it comes every week."

"It comes every week," Naomi echoed, nodding her head vigorously.

"The rabbis of old regarded the Sabbath as the most important Jewish holy day," their father said, "and many Jews still regard it so. One of our wise leaders of modern times, Ahad Ha'am, said, 'The Jews have not only kept the Sabbath, but the Sabbath has kept the Jews.' By this he meant that as long as Jews observe this one day each week, they will remain a united people and never forget that they are Jews."

Aunt Elsa got up to help the maid bring in the next course, and conversation was forgotten for awhile as they all enjoyed the golden chicken soup. Then Dr. Jonathon came back to his subject. "Do you know," he told them, "that the idea of a weekly day of rest was given to the world by the Jews. They were the first among ancient peoples to observe such a day. The Jewish Sabbath began —let's see—more than three thousand years ago."

"It must be pretty old," Maury interrupted, "because

it's in the Ten Commandments and those date back to the time of Moses."

"The Fourth Commandment," added Aunt Elsa. " 'Remember the Sabbath day and keep it holy. Six days shalt thou labor and do all thy work. But the seventh day is the Sabbath of the Lord thy God. On it thou shalt not do any work, neither thou, nor thy son, nor thy daughter, nor thy man-servant, nor thy maid-servant, nor thine ox, nor thy donkey, nor the stranger that is within thy gates.' " She paused a little breathlessly. "There's more to it, but I won't try to quote it all by heart."

"You've done very well," cried Dr. Jonathon approvingly. "You and Maury have both proven my point about the Sabbath being a very old Jewish holy day."

"I can prove it too," cried Ruthie eagerly. "The Bible tells us that when Moses led the Jews out of Egypt and they wandered in the wilderness, God sent them manna for food. And on Fridays, the Jews were told to gather twice as much so they wouldn't have to work on Saturday, which was the day of rest. And that's why we have two loaves of bread on the table—to represent the double portion of manna."

"What a well-informed family I have," said her father proudly.

"We just studied about the Sabbath in the Synagogue School," Ruthie confessed.

"Well, I'm glad the Jews thought of the idea of a Sabbath day for the world," Aunt Elsa put in. "If I didn't get one day's vacation from shopping and cooking, I don't know what I'd do."

"Wouldn't it be awful if people had to work seven days a week and didn't have a day of rest!" Ruthie was overcome at the thought.

"There are lots of people all around us who don't have a Sabbath day," her father reminded her. "The Sabbath is like a shy guest. When she isn't invited and made welcome, she doesn't come."

"She doesn't come to Judy's house," Ruthie said a bit sadly. "That's why Judy loves to come here on Friday nights and on Saturday afternoons. May I invite her for supper next Friday night, mother?"

"Of course," Mrs. Jonathon agreed. "You know that we like to follow the old Jewish custom of having a guest on Friday night, especially someone who doesn't have a Sabbath at home, or who is a stranger in the town."

"Judy will be so glad," cried Ruth delightedly.

"Being an only child is hard on Judy," Mrs. Jonathon said gently. "No wonder she's lonely. You'll have to invite her here more often."

"Talking about welcoming the Sabbath," Dr. Jonathon said, "reminds me of an interesting description in the Talmud which tells how the Sabbath was welcomed in Palestine in those far-off days. Some of the rabbis would dress themselves in their Sabbath clothes and actually go out to meet the Sabbath. Late on Friday afternoon, they would form a procession and go outside the town, chanting psalms and singing, 'Come, let us go forth and meet the Sabbath Queen. Welcome, Sabbath Bride.' "

"I like that," cried Ruthie. "It makes you think of the Sabbath as a sort of lovely angel who comes to visit once a week."

"In modern Palestine, the Sabbath day is also observed in interesting ways," her father continued. "Of course, the ordinary work of the week stops, for the main principle

of the Sabbath day is rest. Jewish stores, offices, and fac-
tories are closed. In the all-Jewish city of Tel Aviv, even
government offices do not open on *Shabbat*. There is practically no traffic on the streets, for buses and taxis do not
run from sunset on Friday to Saturday evening. So even
outdoors one gets the Sabbath feeling of peace and quiet.

"The pleasant custom of bringing fresh flowers into the
home in honor of the Sabbath is observed very widely in
Palestine. Friday is a very busy day for florists. And, of
course, in almost every home the Sabbath candles are lit.

"After the evening meal, young people meet their
friends and go strolling through the streets, singing songs.
In many homes, groups of friends gather to spend the
evening together, talking or singing."

"It sounds very pleasant," Mrs. Jonathon said. "Here
in the United States we have to work so much harder to
feel the presence of the shy Sabbath Queen. But she must
feel quite at home in Palestine."

"Let's sing some songs ourselves now, while we are
waiting for dessert," Maury suggested. And so they sang
their beloved *Friday night songs,* as Ruthie called them.

After dessert had been eaten and grace said, the family
gathered in the living room. Simon forgot that just a few
hours ago he had been lonely and unhappy. He was glad
that tonight Dr. Jonathon wouldn't be hurrying away to

a meeting or working in his office. Aunt Elsa wouldn't be busy with household duties or dashing off to a committee meeting of her club.

"It's nice being home on Friday nights," he said contentedly.

"Oh, Simon," laughed his aunt affectionately, "you're such a homeloving boy. Maury, here, is never happy unless he's dashing around."

"Except on Friday nights," Maury protested. "I never mind being home then. Especially when I have a nice new book on photography," and he opened it immediately.

"When I was a boy," Dr. Jonathon began, and all the children gathered around him eagerly, while Maury promptly closed his book. "The Sabbath was a great day in our little village in Lithuania." Their father's voice took on that dreamy sound it always did when he spoke about his boyhood. "Everyone looked forward to it all week. School closed at noon on Friday. At home, Friday was the busiest day of the week. What cleaning and scrubbing there went on! Everything had to be bright and shining for the Sabbath. The kitchen would be filled with delicious odors. I can see mother rolling out the thin golden sheet of dough for the noodles, her arms floury up to the elbows.

"When the candles were lit at sunset, a wonderful feeling of peace and contentment descended over the house,

over the entire village. Care and worries were banished. When father came in from the synagogue there was a look of good cheer upon his face and he completely forgot that business had been very poor all week. Perhaps he was thinking about the beautiful legend which says that God sends two angels to accompany every Jew from the synagogue to his home on Friday night. After wishing us all a 'Good Sabbath,' he would chant that lovely song, *Shalom Aleihem,* 'Peace to Thee.'

"After the meal, father often told us stories about the Sabbath. My favorite legend was about the river Sambatyon."

"Tell us, daddy," pleaded Ruthie.

"The Sambatyon was a great river which flowed for six days and was dry on the Sabbath. Beyond this river, in a land of peace and prosperity, there was a Jewish kingdom. The Ten Lost Tribes of Israel lived there, safe from every enemy. For this mighty Sambatyon poured forth a stream of rocks and gravel so swiftly and fiercely that none would dare to cross it. And on the Sabbath day, when the river rested, a heavy fog would descend over it so that no one could see it."

"That's a nice story," said Naomi.

"Were you sorry when the Sabbath was over?" Maury asked. He was always tremendously interested in hearing about the days when his father was a boy.

"Yes," Dr. Jonathon nodded. "Around twilight on Saturday, a spirit of sadness seemed to creep into the air. The work and worries of the everyday world would soon begin again. When father came home from the synagogue, he recited the Havdoloh prayer over a cup of wine, just as I do now. Then the atmosphere became more cheerful and we sang songs about the coming of the great prophet, Elijah, just as we do here."

"Why about Elijah?" Simon wanted to know

"Well, there is an old belief that some day Elijah will come and lead all the Jewish people back to the Promised Land. Of course, Elijah is never expected on a Saturday. Therefore, right after the Havdoloh ceremony, which marks the departure of the Sabbath, one may again look forward to the coming of the great prophet."

On Saturday morning, the Jonathon family went to the synagogue. Simon liked to hear the cantor, who chanted the prayers so beautifully. He also liked the parts in the service when the silk curtains of the Ark were drawn aside. Then the whole congregation rose in reverence as the scrolls of the Torah were revealed, resting against the back wall of the Ark. Several times during the service, Simon looked up at the light which hung above the Ark. It was called the Eternal Light, the *Ner Tomid*. This light is never permitted to go out, as long as a synagogue stands, for it is a symbol of the eternal light of Judaism. In ancient

times, the Eternal Light burned in the Temple at Jerusalem. Each Ner Tomid in the hundreds of thousands of
synagogues all over the world proves that the light of
Judaism continues to burn from the ancient past to the
present.

An important part of the Sabbath morning service is
the reading from the Torah. Simon watched with interest
when the rabbi reverently lifted a scroll from the Ark and
laid it upon the reading desk which stood upon the platform. The rabbi took off the silver ornaments which decorated the tops of the wooden handles of the scroll. Then he
removed the embroidered velvet covering and the white
band beneath, with which the scroll was tied. He unrolled
the scroll to the correct portion for that week. Various
members of the congregation were called up to the pulpit
to recite a blessing before and after each section of the
Torah that was read. At least seven men are called upon
each Sabbath morning for this honor. Simon felt proud
when Dr. Jonathon was one of them.

A scroll of the Torah contains the *Five Books of Moses,*
which are the first five books of the Bible. They are also
called the *Pentateuch,* from the Greek word meaning *five
books.* Each scroll is written by hand on heavy parchment
with a quill pen and a special kind of ink. It takes a long
time to write a scroll of Torah. The writer, or scribe, must
be a learned man and must work slowly and carefully. If

he makes a single mistake, the entire scroll cannot be used. The scroll is mounted on wooden rollers. As you have heard, it is decorated with a velvet covering and generally has silver ornaments on the tops of the scrolls. A silver hand for pointing is attached to the scroll by a cord.

Every Sabbath morning a portion of the Torah is read in the synagogue. During the course of the year, the entire *Five Books* are read.

After the reading from the Torah, a portion from another scroll, containing the books of the prophets, also from the Bible, is read. This part is known as the *Haftorah,* which means the *reading before dismissal.* When a boy becomes Bar Mitzvah he is called upon to read the Haftorah for that particular week.

After the closing hymn and the rabbi's benediction, the Jonathon family walked slowly homeward. Maury tried to hurry the others along. He was eager for the Sabbath dinner to begin, for his father had promised to let him recite the Kiddush and to lead in the saying of grace afterwards.

Maury chanted the Kiddush very nicely. Simon wondered if he would ever be able to do as well. In the saying of grace, too, Maury seldom stumbled over the Hebrew words.

"Very good," his father cried approvingly.

"It ought to be," Maury answered, a bit grumblingly. "I

spend enough time studying it." But they all knew he felt pleased and proud.

"I shall enjoy my nap this afternoon," Dr. Jonathon declared as they arose from the table. "I've had such a busy week, I haven't had time to catch my breath. Come, Naomi. I'll tuck you away at the same time."

"Goody," cried Naomi. Having daddy tuck her away meant a half hour of fun first.

"And I'm going to get into my housecoat and settle down with my new book," Aunt Elsa said happily. "I've been looking forward to that all week. How about you children?"

"Let's go for a walk in the park," Ruthie suggested. "It's a lovely day."

"Sorry," Maury started towards the door. "Our club is having a discussion group this afternoon. It's going to be exciting, too. Want to come, Simon?"

"Sure thing." Simon was enthusiastic.

"What about me?" Ruthie's voice was very forlorn.

"Oh, all right, you can come too," Maury agreed. "These Saturday afternoon meetings are open to the public and we can bring friends."

The short Sabbath afternoon sped away all too quickly. Dr. Jonathon went to attend the brief services held in the synagogue about sunset. When he returned it was dark and everyone was home, waiting for Havdoloh. This cere-

mony marks the end of the Sabbath and the beginning of
the working week. Dr. Jonathon filled his goblet with
wine. Ruth had the privilege of holding the long braided
Havdoloh candle. Naomi held the lovely silver spice box
filled with fragrant spices. The Hebrew prayer of Havdoloh which their father chanted gave thanks to God
for the good things of life, such as the Sabbath day, for
light and joy and gladness and honor. He paused at one
point and raised the spice-box to his face, smelling its
fragrance, for on the joyous Sabbath, the sense of smell,
too, should be gladdened. "Blessed art thou, O Lord our
God, King of the Universe, who createst various kinds
of spices," he was saying. Then, in the light of the candle,
he bent his fingers over the palm of his hand, causing a
shadow to fall, and thus showing the difference between
light and darkness as he continued, "Blessed art Thou,
O Lord our God, who createst the light of the fire.
Blessed art thou, O Lord our God, King of the Universe,
who makest a distinction between holy and ordinary, between light and darkness, between Israel and other nations, between the seventh day and the six working days.
Blessed art thou, O Lord, who makest a distinction between the holy and the ordinary."

After the ceremony, they all sang the song customary
among Jews on this occasion, about Elijah the prophet.
It was Ruthie's favorite melody and she loved to sing it in

the soft light of the Havdoloh candle, as the family stood gathered together in a small group. When the electric lights were finally flashed on and the greetings, "A good week," exchanged, there was something of regret among them for a precious moment that had passed. But, already, they could look forward to the coming of the next Sabbath day.

THINGS TO DO AND TALK ABOUT
THE SABBATH

Reviewing the Story

1. What part does Aunt Elsa have in the preparation of the Sabbath? In the ceremonies of the Sabbath?
2. What customs and ceremonies does Uncle Phil observe on Friday evening?
3. How does the whole family share in the spirit of the Sabbath eve?
4. What interesting things did you learn about the history of the Sabbath day?
5. What does Uncle Phil mean by saying the Sabbath is like a shy guest? Do you agree with him?
6. Describe how the Sabbath is celebrated in Tel Aviv.
7. What did you find especially interesting in Uncle Phil's description of how he used to spend the Sabbath day when he was a boy in Lithuania?
8. How do the Jonathons and Simon spend the Sabbath day?
9. What objects are needed to observe the Havdoloh ceremony? What is the purpose of this ceremony?
10. Why are songs about Elijah generally sung after Havdoloh?

For Classroom Conversation

1. Why is it difficult for many families in the United States to observe the Sabbath day in the traditional way?
2. Do you think that many families could keep the Sabbath day to a greater extent, if they made the effort? Do you think it would be desirable for them to do so? Discuss.
3. In what ways do you think the Sabbath day could be made to mean more to the average American Jewish family?

4. Tell what you will try to do to make the Sabbath day more meaningful in your own home.

5. Tell how various Jewish families whom you know, observe the Sabbath day.

Suggested Activities

Giving a Play—The story of *The Sabbath* which you have just read is dramatized for you in the following pages. Put on this play in your classroom or for a school assembly. If you haven't time to do this, read the play aloud in class.

THE SABBATH DAY

Scene One

SIMON's *room: The usual sort of boy's room in a middle-class family.* SIMON *is sitting on a chair at one end of the stage, turning the leaves of a magazine with a bored air. He shows by his manner that he is not too pleased at the way life is treating him.*

RUTHIE: (*Heard off stage.*) Si-mon, Si-mon, where are you? (*Bursts into his room.*) Oh, there you are! What are you doing, Simon?

SIMON: (*Crossly.*) Not a thing! What is there to do? This is the most vanishing family I've ever seen. Maury's in the dark room fooling with his photography. Of course, Uncle Phil is busy. I don't see Aunt Elsa anywhere around. And even you managed to disappear.

RUTHIE: (*Smiling a little.*) Poor Simon. I think you're lonely.

SIMON: (*Still crossly.*) No, I'm not. But I guess I've got a right to miss my mother and dad once in a while. Rio de Janeiro is pretty far away, you know.

RUTHIE: (*Sympathetically.*) Of course it is. I understand, Simon.

SIMON: (*In a more friendly tone.*) When we have a lot of holidays, it's different. Then everybody's home and it's nice and jolly. Friday nights are nice too—and Saturdays. But during the week, everybody's always so busy.

RUTHIE: You're pretty busy yourself, most of the time, Simon. But I don't know why you're cross today if you like Fridays.

SIMON: But today isn't—

RUTHIE: (*Opens the door leading to the hall.*) Come over here. What do you smell?

(*They both sniff the air.*)

SIMON: (*Happily.*) Honeycake! Oh, boy! I don't know why I kept thinking it was Thursday all day. Gee, that means everybody will be home tonight.

RUTHIE: It's Friday, all right, Mr. Absent-minded Professor. And that reminds me—I was looking for you to help me arrange the flowers for the table. Mother got some beautiful ones this week.

SIMON: (*Cheerfully.*) Then what are we standing here for? Let's get going.

(*They go out and the curtain closes.*)

Scene Two

The dining room of the JONATHON *home. The table is set for the Sabbath meal.* AUNT ELSA *comes in with two candles in her hand and places them in the silver candlesticks which are standing on the table.* UNCLE PHIL *enters from another door, humming a little tune. He is buttoning his suit coat, then he fixes his tie, and straightens the handkerchief in his breast pocket.*

UNCLE PHIL: I'm sorry I couldn't get away from the office in time for synagogue this evening. I had a houseful of patients. Am I glad this is Friday night!

AUNT ELSA: Me, too. I feel as if I've been rushing madly around all week. What with committee meetings, Red Cross work, and all— Call the children, please, Phil. It's time to light the candles. Ruthie and Naomi would never forgive me if I lit the candles without their being here. (*There is a sound of voices outside.*) Oh, here they come now.

(MAURY, SIMON, RUTHIE, *and* NAOMI *all come in.*)

RUTHIE: I've collected everybody for you, mother.

MAURY: You? Or was it the delicious odors from the kitchen? They act like a magnet, mother. I felt myself irresistibly drawn in this direction. We've been studying about magnets in our science class, but one rule I've had to discover for myself is this: (*Recites as one would a lesson.*) When the delicious odor of Mrs. Jonathon's cooking reaches a certain point of intensity, the magnetic field extends to the darkened photography room at the other end of the hall. A series of ether waves are set in motion. Result: Maury Jonathon makes a bee-line for the dining room.

(*Everybody laughs.*)

AUNT ELSA: I'm ready to light the candles now, children.

(*She strikes a match and lights them. She spreads her hands over the flames, then holds her hands before her face and recites the blessing, first in Hebrew and then in English.* (See page 229)

(*Everyone sings the song welcoming the Sabbath, first in Hebrew, then in English.* (See page 229) DR. JONATHON *looks affectionately at his wife and recites some verses from the* Book of Proverbs. (See page 69) *Then he blesses each member of the family.* (See page 229) *They gather around the table.* DR. JONATHON *recites the Kiddush, and then all are seated. He repeats the blessing over the bread and the meal is begun.* (See pages 226 and 229))

(*The conversation during the meal, which is about the Sabbath day, can be taken directly from the story.* (Pages 72–77) *Afterwards, there should be the singing of Friday night songs. The scene ends with the saying of grace. The curtain could be lowered as the chanting of the grace begins.* (Page 234)

Scene Three

(*This scene may be omitted if the time for preparation is limited.*)

In the living room, Friday night, after dinner. Follow the conversation in the story. (Pages 78–81) *If you wish to make this scene longer, add more stories and legends about the Sabbath.*

Scene Four

In the JONATHON *living room. It is twilight, on Saturday.* UNCLE PHIL, *seated in an armchair, puts down a book which he has been reading by the fading daylight.* AUNT ELSA, *dressed in a housecoat, comes in, stifling a yawn.*

AUNT ELSA: Are you still reading, Phil? I had the grandest nap.

UNCLE PHIL: (*Laughing.*) It seems to me, we started the afternoon with *you* reading and *me* taking the nap.

AUNT ELSA: Then it's quite natural to end it this way, isn't it? Well, anyhow, it's been a good day.

(*A rather noisy tramping of feet and loud voices are heard outside.*)

UNCLE PHIL: Am I mistaken, or do I hear the patter of little feet?

AUNT ELSA: Sounds more like a stampede to me.

(RUTHIE's *high shrill voice is heard offstage, getting louder as the children approach.*)

RUTHIE: I did, too, have a right to take part in the discussion, Maury Jonathon. And the leader said my argument was good, too. And he was pleased with the story I told about Akiba and Rachel. (*The last sentence is said as the children enter the living room.*)

MAURY: (*Good-naturedly.*) All right, all right. I was merely pointing out, my dear and brilliant sister, that as a guest at our discussion club, it wasn't quite the thing to monopolize the conversation. Oh, hello, mother, hello, dad. Hardly saw you in the dark.

UNCLE PHIL: (*Pleasantly.*) Well, we didn't have any trouble *hearing* you. Neither did the neighbors, I'm sure. It's time for Havdoloh. Where is Naomi?

NAOMI: (*Entering.*) Here she is. And I have the Havdoloh candle all ready, daddy.

UNCLE PHIL: That's fine.

RUTHIE: I'll get the spice box. (*She does so.*)

AUNT ELSA: (*Bringing in a bottle of wine and a goblet.*) Here is the wine and Havdoloh cup.

UNCLE PHIL: All right, I think we're all ready.

(*Everyone gathers around* UNCLE PHIL. *He lights the long, braided candle which Naomi is holding. Then he fills the goblet with wine and recites the Havdoloh.* (See page 231) *Afterwards, the group sings* "Eliyahu, Hanavi." *The electric lights are flashed on. Greetings for a good week are exchanged, the curtain falls.*)

HANUKAH

O H, Simon, you were a wonderful Judah Maccabee. I felt so proud of you," Ruthie said admiringly.

"Oh, Simon, you were wonderful," cried little Naomi, clinging to her brother Maury with one hand and tightly clutching a gaily-colored box of Hanukah candy with the other. The four children were on their way home from the Synagogue School, where they had enjoyed a Hanukah celebration. The air was crisp and the newly-fallen snow sparkled in the sunlight. Simon's eyes were still glowing with the excitement of being the hero of the play.

"It was such fun," he said. "Why, several times I felt as if I were really Judah Maccabee, leading my victorious soldiers into Jerusalem. The re-dedication of the Temple was exciting too."

"You spoke the lines well," Maury told him, and Simon felt a glow of pleasure, for Maury's words of praise were seldom given and meant much to the younger boy.

95

"I feel as if this were my first Hanukah," he remarked as they trudged along. "In our little town back home, the few Jewish families didn't pay much attention to this festival."

"Didn't your daddy even light the Hanukah lights in the Menorah?" Ruth asked unbelievingly.

"No." Simon's tone was regretful. "But after this I'm going to ask him to," he declared.

"We'd better hurry," Maury reminded them, "because our Hanukah party will start early this afternoon."

"This is certainly a swell day." Simon kicked up the soft snow enthusiastically as he walked.

"Mother always lets us have a Hanukah party," Ruth told him.

At the dinner table, the talk was still about Hanukah. "This festival stands for a great ideal," Dr. Jonathon told them. "Jews were probably the first people in the world to fight for religious freedom. And that was pretty long ago—'way back in 165 B. C."

"But what I still can't understand," Ruthie's tone was puzzled, "is why that foolish old king, Antiochus Epiphanes, was so determined to make the Jews give up their religion and worship the Greek gods."

"Well, you see," her father explained, "the Syrian kingdom over which Antiochus ruled, was made up of many different nationalities, each with its own religion. Antiochus thought that he would strengthen his empire if he could unite the people under one religion. And so he ordered all his subjects to worship the Greek gods, for he had been brought up as a Greek."

"I guess he didn't understand the Jews very well if he thought they would give up their religion so easily," Maury put in.

"He was a very stubborn man with a bad temper, always determined to have his own way," Dr. Jonathon replied. "No wonder they called him the *Madman*. Antiochus sent his large, well-trained army into Palestine to force the stubborn Jews to obey his decrees. Greek gods were set up in the Temple. The holy altar was made impure by the sacrifice of unclean animals. The Jews were forbidden on penalty of death to practice their religion. Finally, the Maccabean family organized a revolt."

"In the village of Modin," put in Ruthie, "where Mattathias and his five sons lived."

"Yes," her father nodded. "And one of the sons, Judah Maccabee, became the leader. The Jews fought bravely against their stronger foe. And although they were small in number and ill-trained, the Jewish soldiers won a great victory. You see, they were fighting for something more precious to them than life—the right to live in freedom.

"For three whole years," Dr. Jonathon continued, "the capital city, Jerusalem, and the holy Temple, were in the hands of the enemy. And then, after a great battle, the road to the city was cleared, and the Jewish army re-entered Jerusalem. You can imagine with what joy they were greeted. One of their first tasks was to restore the Temple to order, so that services might be held there again.

"The entire events of Hanukah are related in *The Book of the Maccabees,* which was written in ancient times, shortly after these events took place. We are given a very clear picture of what the Temple looked like when Judah Maccabee and his soldiers took it from the enemy. I was reading this description just the other day. Although it was written over two thousand years ago, I could imagine I was there with those men and could feel what they felt when they saw the condition of their beloved Temple. The once-glorious structure with its splendid courtyards was in a state of terrible neglect. The huge gates, once decorated with burnished copper which had sparkled in the sunlight, had been pulled down and destroyed. In the spacious courtyards, which had been tiled with fine marble, shrubs were growing as in a forest. The chambers where the priests had lived were pulled down. But saddest of all was the sight of the great altar of burnt offerings. On it, un-clean animals had been sacrificed to Greek gods.

"When the Jews beheld these things, they wept with grief. But they set to work at once to restore the Temple to order. They wondered what to do about the great altar.

Could it be made clean and pure again? They decided that it couldn't. And so it was torn down and a new one was built in its place. The whole Temple was cleaned and repaired. New utensils needed in the sacrifices were made. The large, seven-branched candlestick was placed in the Temple again and was lighted. All was made ready for services to be restored. And then came the happy day of the re-dedication of the Temple. How the people rejoiced and gave thanks to God! This re-dedication of the Temple meant that the Jewish people were once more free to worship God in their own way. It meant that they could live freely as Jews. This great occasion was celebrated for eight days. Ever since that time, Jews have observed this holiday of dedication—Hanukah."

"And the first Hanukah really happened over two thousand years ago," Simon remarked thoughtfully.

"And we are going to celebrate it this afternoon with a party," Ruthie marveled.

"Yes," agreed Aunt Elsa, "and there are still some things to do before our guests arrive."

Soon it was three o'clock. In the large, cheerful living room, a jolly crowd of children was gathered. The furniture had been pushed against the wall to make room for games.

"We are going to play charades and pantomimes," Mrs. Jonathon announced. "In the past, many communities used to celebrate Hanukah by having plays and masquerades, just as they did at Purim."

"We have plays, too," one of the children said. "We had one this morning in religious school."

"That's right," Mrs. Jonathon agreed. "So you see, this game we are going to play is very fitting for Hanukah. Every word you act out must be connected with the story of Hanukah."

The children formed into small groups and amid much chattering and giggling, chose their words and the action which would describe them. Some of the most popular words which the children acted out were *Maccabee, Modin,* and *Menorah.* Bobby, one of the guests, won a prize for a pantomime. He had begged an old sheet from Mrs. Jonathon. This was draped around him and tied with a sash. Flourishing a yardstick in one hand, he cried out, "All who are zealous for the Lord, follow me."

"Mattathias, Mattathias," cried the children delightedly.

"That's right," Bobby nodded. "He was the father of Judah Maccabee."

"I want to direct the next game," Dr. Jonathon announced. "It is one that is always associated with the Hanukah festival."

"I know," cried Ruthie. "It's spinning the top. That's lots of fun."

Her father produced a number of tops, each having four wings. On each wing was printed one of the four Hebrew letters, *nun* (N), *gimmel* (G), *he* (H), and *shin* (SH). "The letters stand for the Hebrew words, *Nes Godol Hoyoh Shom, A Great Miracle Happened There,*" Dr. Jonathon explained.

"I guess you mean about the cruse of oil," Mary, one of the guests, cried out.

"Tell us the story," Mrs. Jonathon suggested.

"Oh, everybody knows it, I guess," Mary replied. "There is a legend that when Judah Maccabee and his soldiers cleaned up the Temple and rebuilt the altar which the Greeks had defiled, they were ready to re-dedicate the Temple. But they had no pure oil with which to light the Menorah. Finally, they found one small flask of pure oil. There was just enough to last one day. But *A Great Miracle Happened There,* according to the story, and the oil burned for eight days, until more could be brought."

"The rabbis of long ago said that this was the reason why Hanukah, the Festival of Lights, is celebrated eight days," Mrs. Jonathon added.

"Now let's go on with the game," Ruthie said.

"There are several ways of playing it," her father explained. "See, you spin it, like this. Whether you win or lose depends on what letter is on the face of the top when it falls. *N* stands for *Nothing, G* stands for *Goal,* or all of the pot, *H* stands for *Half,* and *SH* means *Shove,* or put more into the pot."

"But what will we play with?" asked Ruthie.

"Here." Dr. Jonathon opened a small sack and poured out a stream of golden walnuts. Each child received twenty-five.

What fun it was! What merriment and excitement were aroused as the game progressed. Simon thought it was the jolliest party he had ever attended.

"I've lost all mine," Maury said ruefully, after a while.

"Look at my pile." Simon pointed to it proudly. "I guess I've won the most."

"And now it is time to light the Hanukah candles," Dr. Jonathon said. On the wide window-sill he placed a beautiful Menorah made of silver. After lighting the first candle, he called on some of the children, and each one stepped up to the Menorah and lit one candle. Then Dr. Jonathon recited the blessing, first in Hebrew and then in English. "Blessed art Thou, O Lord our God, King of the Universe, who has sanctified us by thy commandments and commanded us to kindle the Hanukah lights." Everyone sang *Rock of Ages* while Mrs. Jonathon softly accompanied them on the piano. In the dusk, the candles gleamed brightly.

"Time for refreshments," the hostess announced. As the children entered the dining room, they cried out with

admiration and delight. In the center of the table stood a huge chocolate cake on which was inscribed in white letters, *Happy Hanukah*. Two tall blue candles, one at each end of the table, cast a soft light. With much merriment, the children moved around, trying to find their names on the attractive little place-cards which were in the form of Menorahs.

"Oh, look," cried Bobby, picking up one of the small boxes which were set in each place. He poured the contents into his hand—a stream of shining new pennies.

"You know," Dr. Jonathon told him smilingly, "it is the custom on Hanukah to give children *Hanukah-money*. As a boy, I always looked forward to that event. So I gave each of you twenty pennies."

First, potato pancakes were served. "It is the custom," Mrs. Jonathon told her guests, "to eat pancakes on Hanukah." Ice-cream, cake, and candy followed next. There was a happy silence for a while. Everyone was too busy to talk.

Then Bobby had a sudden inspiration. "Say, Dr. Jonathon, don't you think we could give these pennies to the Jewish Welfare Fund?"

"Yes, let's," several of the others chimed in.

"A very fine idea," Dr. Jonathon agreed. "You might give it through your religious school fund. Here, Simon, pass this box around and those who wish to, can put in as many of their pennies as they like."

"I know what we ought to do now," Maury suggested. "We ought to get father to tell us how he used to celebrate Hanukah in the days when he was a boy."

"Yes, yes, please do," a dozen voices chorused, and so Dr. Jonathon agreed.

"It was a holiday which we children in the small village of Lithuania loved dearly, and we looked forward to its arrival with much anticipation," he began. It came in the bitter, cold days of winter, when the snow was thick upon the ground. The holidays of the fall season had been long forgotten, and we boys in the Heder, as our Hebrew school was called, were beginning to get very weary of our regular lessons. Hanukah was a happy change for us. In the first place, we had school for only half days during all of the eight days of the festival. And even during the time we were in school, there was not much serious studying going on. We played games, chiefly *Spinning the Top,* and listened to stories which the teacher told us. He used to change remarkably during holiday seasons, and the whole atmosphere of the Heder was different. Why, even before Hanukah arrived, his stern expression would soften and he would even smile once in a while. He didn't use his leather strap quite as frequently. And when he told us Hanukah stories, the frown on his brow would clear up and his eyes would shine with a happy light. After hearing about Mattathias and Judah Maccabee, we youngsters would strut around with wooden swords, as if we were the heroes.

"At home, we looked forward to the lighting of the first

candle in the Hanukah Menorah. After father recited the blessing, we all sang songs. Then came a special supper, with all sorts of good things to eat. After the meal, we spent the evening playing games, telling stories, and singing. Those were jolly times, all right.

"I always enjoyed seeing another little golden candle being added to the Menorah each night. The fifth night was a special occasion. That was when our relatives came over and spent the evening with us. We received our *Hanukah-money* then, and mother would serve delicious pancakes and other goodies."

"We always got our *Hanukah-money* right through the festival," Mrs. Jonathon put in. "On the night of the first candle, we would get one bright, new penny, on the second night, two pennies, and so on."

"You must have come from a wealthier home than I," smiled her husband.

It was time for the guests to leave now, but one could tell by their happy faces that they had enjoyed their Hanukah party.

THINGS TO DO AND TALK ABOUT
HANUKAH

Reviewing the Story

1. What does the word *Hanukah* mean? Why is it a fitting name for this festival?
2. Who are the main persons in the historic events of Hanukah? Discuss each of these people, telling what qualities of character they had and on what you base your opinion.
3. For what ideal were the Jews fighting when they rebelled against the Syrians?
4. Describe the appearance of the Temple in Jerusalem when Judah Maccabee and his soldiers finally re-conquered the city.
5. What special ceremony is performed each day of the Hanukah festival?
6. In what ancient book is the story of Hanukah told?
7. What legend explains why Hanukah is celebrated for eight days?
8. What are some of the customs which children, particularly, enjoy during this holiday?

For Classroom Conversation

1. Do you think the Hanukah story has any special meaning for us today? Discuss.
2. Do you know of any other struggles for the ideal of religious liberty, both in the past or in the present, by Jews or other groups?

3. In what great document has the United States made safe
for its people the right to freedom of worship? Bring this
document to class and read the section about religious
liberty.
4. Tell how Hanukah is celebrated in your home. What plans
are you making to celebrate it this year? Or, if the holiday is past, how did you celebrate it?

Suggested Activities

1.

Plan a Hanukah party like the one described in the story.
Make place-cards for the table, using Hanukah symbols. Paint
large pictures to decorate the room. Make tops for playing *Spinning the Top*. If you have time, prepare a Hanukah play to present at the party. Make up original Hanukah poems. Learn
Hanukah songs.

2.

Make a Hanukah Menorah as a gift for your parents. It can
be made out of clay or wood.

THE JEWISH HOME

BAR MITZVAH

THIS vacation is certainly going to be different from what I had planned," Judy said to Simon, looking out of the train window at the thickly falling snow. "I was so excited about spending this week with the Jonathons. Ruthie and I have been talking about it for days and days. And then they all had to go and get the measles!"

"You ought to be glad Aunt Elsa didn't decide to call your mother and father back from Florida to take care of you," Simon replied. "As things are, we'll probably have fun, anyhow. Aunt Bess and Uncle David are grand, and so is grandfather."

"It was good of them to let me come, considering that I'm a perfect stranger to them," Judy said seriously, a thoughtful look in her brown eyes. "Especially since this is going to be such a busy week for Aunt Bess, with Danny being Bar Mitzvah next Saturday."

"It's a shame the Jonathons will have to miss the Bar Mitzvah," Simon remarked, "but I'm glad they are not very ill. They all have mild cases, the doctor said. And don't you worry about Aunt Bess," he went on comfortingly. "She loves taking care of people and she'll make you feel at home in no time.

"Here we are already. I see Uncle David on the platform." Simon felt very grown-up as he got the two suitcases down from the rack above the seat and struggled between them towards the door.

"Here, let me have those," Uncle David called as he caught sight of them descending the train steps, aided by the conductor's friendly hand. "My car is right here. How are you, Simon, my boy? And this, I suppose, is Judy."

"Yes, Uncle David. Judy, this is Uncle David." The two shook hands, smiled at each other, and were friends immediately. Simon was glad the little girl was not shy and made friends so easily.

"What is that funny little metal case on the doorpost?" Judy asked promptly, when they reached the house.

"I would lose my key on a night like this!" Uncle David's voice was a bit cross as he put down the second suitcase and turned up the collar of his coat against the wetness of the falling snow. "What's that you're saying, Judy?" He continued to search in his pockets as he spoke. "Oh, that's a Mezuzah. Don't tell me you've never seen one!

"Well, thank goodness," he exclaimed in relief as he finally discovered the key hidden between the pages of his small address book. "Aunt Bess is going to be a little late," he told the children as they entered the warm, cozy apartment and he switched on the lights in the living room.

"I guess Danny's Bar Mitzvah is keeping her pretty busy," Simon remarked.

"Terribly busy," said a gay voice behind him. His pretty auntie swept into the room and enfolded him in a hug. Her voice was so warm with welcome that Simon didn't mind the coldness of the snow that was clinging to her fur coat. "Hello, Judy," she turned to the little girl and put an arm around her. "We hope you will have a happy visit with us."

"Hi, Simon," Danny shouted, "mother bought me a new suit today for the Bar Mitzvah. It's a whiz."

"In just a few minutes, I'll feed my hungry family." Aunt Bess had taken off her wraps and slipped an apron over her dress. "This is Mary's afternoon off, but she has the table set and the dinner cooked."

"Uncle David," Simon reminded him as they sat down in the living room to wait, "you didn't tell Judy about that little metal case on the doorpost—the Mez—what did you call it?"

"The Mezuzah," his uncle told him. "It is placed on the doorposts of Jewish homes. I'm sure there is one on Uncle Phil's."

"I guess I didn't happen to notice it," Simon admitted. "Tell us about it."

"First of all, the Mezuzah is a sign that a Jewish family lives within the house upon whose doorpost it is nailed. The word *Mezuzah* comes from the Hebrew word meaning *doorpost*. The Mezuzah case contains a small scroll of parchment on which several passages from the Bible are written in tiny Hebrew letters. The first six verses are from Deuteronomy, Chapter Six. I am sure you would recognize them if I recited them for you."

"Please do, Uncle David," Judy begged.

"Very well," he agreed. "Here they are.

'Hear O Israel, the Lord our God, the Lord is one.
And thou shalt love the Lord thy God with all thy
    heart, with all thy soul, and with all thy might.
And these words which I command thee this day shall
    be in thy heart.
And thou shalt teach them diligently unto thy chil-
    dren, speaking of them when thou sittest in thy
    house, when thou walkest by the way, when thou
    liest down, and when thou risest up.
And thou shalt bind them for a sign upon thy hand
    and they shall be as frontlets between thine eyes.
And thou shalt write them upon the doorposts of thy
    house and upon thy gates.' "

" 'Upon the doorposts of thy house,' " repeated Simon. "I guess that explains the Mezuzah. But what does that other part mean, 'as a sign upon thy hand and as frontlets between thine eyes'?"

"I'll show you." Danny spoke eagerly. "I'll show them my Bar Mitzvah present from grandfather, dad." He dashed out and came back with an embroidered velvet bag in one hand and a wrapped package in the other. "See," he opened the bag. "Here are the Tefilin." He took out two black narrow leather straps, each with a little square box attached to it. Danny twined one around his left arm, and the other around his forehead, with the small square box in the center.

"These small boxes," he explained, "contain the same verses that are found in the Mezuzah. In this way, we bind them 'as a sign upon the hand and as frontlets between the eyes,' as the commandment tells us to do."

"The Tefilin remind us of the commandments which bind the people of Israel to God," Uncle David told them. "The pious Orthodox Jew wears them during morning prayers, except on the Sabbath and on holidays. You see, on holy days, the Jew has other reminders of his religion and so does not need the Tefilin in order to make him remember. The Tefilin are worn from the time a boy is Bar Mitzvah. The Talis, or prayer-shawl, is worn around the shoulders during prayers, including the Sabbath and holidays. Show them yours, Danny."

Danny unwrapped his package and proudly displayed the beautiful, silk prayer-shawl, which he placed around his shoulders. It was white with dark stripes at each end and fringes along the edges. The fringes in each of the four corners were longer than the others.

"The prayer-shawl is also worn because of a commandment in the Bible," Uncle David said.

"It seems sort of strange to wear one of those Tefilin in the middle of the forehead," Judy remarked, looking at Danny, who was still wearing them.

"In ancient times," Uncle David told her, "people often wore a jewel upon the forehead, as an ornament. The Jew regards God's commandments as his most precious jewel and so he wears them as a 'frontlet between the eyes.' "

"Grandfather should be home by this time," Aunt Bess interrupted as she came in. "I begged him not to go to the synagogue for afternoon services today because the weather is so damp and cold. He can say his prayers at home, if necessary."

"You know how much he loves the synagogue," her husband replied. "The great joy of his life is to sit in the study room and discuss a few pages of the Talmud with a group of his followers."

"There he is now," cried Danny and ran to open the door.

"Well, well," grandfather pinched his cheek. "You're all dressed up in the Talis and Tefilin. I'm glad you like them, and I hope you will wear them regularly after you are Bar Mitzvah."

"Come, father, you must have a plate of hot soup to warm you." Aunt Bess was unbuttoning his coat and removing the muffler from his neck.

"Don't worry, daughter. The cold weather didn't hurt me." He patted her cheek affectionately. "You see, my dear children," he went on, after greeting Simon and Judy, "this is Judaism in practice, for the Torah says, 'Honor thy father and thy mother, that thy days may be long upon the land which the Lord thy God hath given thee.'"

"Come," Aunt Bess pleaded, "the soup is getting cold."

There was silence for awhile as everyone enjoyed the delicious vegetable soup, which was not at all cold.

"What are you looking for, Judy?" Aunt Bess asked as she saw the child's eyes wandering around the table.

"The butter," she explained, "but it doesn't matter."

"We don't serve butter with meat, Judy," Aunt Bess told her. "We keep a kosher home—that means we observe the Jewish dietary laws."

"Oh, I see," Judy replied. "Grandmother's home is the same way. What are some of the dietary laws, Aunt Bess?"

"I should have warned you about Judy," laughed Simon. "She is more of a question box than I am."

"I shall try to explain some of them to you," Aunt Bess replied, "because I think you ought to know about them, Judy.

"In the first place, no milk foods, including cheese or any other product made from milk, are ever served with meat foods. That is why there isn't any butter on the table now. In the Orthodox Jewish home, there are two sets of dishes, silverware, pots and pans, so that these two kinds of foods never come in contact with each other during cooking or serving. I have separate cupboards in the kitchen, where I keep my meat dishes and my milk dishes, so they won't get mixed up. My blue set is for milk meals and my flowered set for meat meals. We also have two sets of silverware, each with a different design so we can keep them apart. And each set is kept in a different drawer."

"Don't forget to tell her," added Danny, "that after eating meat, Orthodox Jews do not eat any milk foods until six hours later. That's to allow the meat foods to be digested," he explained. "But after eating milk foods, one can eat meat shortly afterwards. I guess that's because it doesn't take so long to digest milk products."

"Are there any other Jewish dietary laws?" asked Judy, much interested. "Oh, I know another one," she added before anyone could reply. "It's about bacon and ham."

"Yes," Aunt Bess told her, "certain foods are forbidden according to the Jewish law. Any form of meat made from the flesh of swine, such as pork, ham, or bacon, are in this class. Certain kinds of sea food, such as lobster, oysters, and clams, are also forbidden."

"The biblical law," added Uncle David, "tells us that Jews may eat meat only from animals which both chew their cud and have split hoofs, and only those kinds of fish which have both fins and scales. All others are regarded as unclean."

"There is something very important that you haven't mentioned," Danny added. "Animals used for kosher meat are slaughtered differently. This work must be done by a *shohet,* a man especially trained according to the Jewish law."

"The Jewish method," Uncle David explained, "is considered the most merciful, for it is done with one skilful stroke of the knife."

"Now I know why Jews have their own butcher shops," Judy said. "It's because there are all these special laws about meat—using only certain animals—and having them killed in a special way and all that."

"What are those Hebrew words that are printed on the windows of Jewish meat stores?" asked Simon.

"They are two words meaning *kosher meat,*" Uncle David replied. "Any food prepared according to Jewish dietary laws is called *kosher*. It is a Hebrew word meaning *fit for use*."

"But making the meat kosher has to be completed at home," Danny added, proud to show his knowledge. "Tell Judy about that, mother."

"I see you won't let me skip a thing," laughed his mother. "Well, meat is made kosher at home in the following way: First it is soaked for half an hour in cold water, then it is sprinkled with coarse salt and put on a draining board for an hour. Then the meat is washed in cold, running water to remove the salt and any remaining blood."

"Why do they want to remove the blood?" asked Judy.

"Because blood is the life stream of the animal, and since all life is considered sacred, blood is not used," Uncle David explained.

"But what are the reasons for all these dietary laws?" Simon wanted to know.

"It's very likely," his uncle told him, "that these rules were originally based on laws of hygiene. Our ancestors lived in a hot climate, where foods spoiled easily. They knew that certain foods caused disease. We know today that if pork is not properly cured and well cooked, it may cause *trichinosis*. We know that sea food from impure waters may carry typhoid fever germs. The Jews, therefore, were forbidden to eat these foods."

"Our ancestors," grandfather added, "really believed that 'cleanliness was next to Godliness.' If they were to be a 'holy people,' as the Bible commanded, then their food had to be clean and pure."

"Another purpose of the Jewish dietary laws," Uncle David went on, "was probably to keep the Jews separate from their neighbors, who were idol-worshipers. These laws have also helped to keep the Jews a united people in the many centuries after they left Palestine and lived in many lands.

"But come, we must finish our meal. Then we can say grace and get up from the table."

"Yes," chimed in Danny eagerly. "I want to show Simon my Bar Mitzvah presents."

A few minutes later, the three children were in Danny's room. A gay sight met their eyes. The table, dresser, and chair were covered with newly-opened boxes and packages. Simon caught his breath at the exciting display of gifts—books, ties, a pocket-knife, a wrist-watch, a camera, and other things.

"It's more fun than regular birthdays or even Hanukah," Danny declared as he proudly displayed his treasures.

By Saturday morning, Simon and Judy were as excited about Danny's Bar Mitzvah as Danny himself. It was Judy's first visit to an Orthodox synagogue and she was

deeply interested in everything she saw. She liked the
warmth and friendliness of the people. She liked to watch
the men praying earnestly as they swayed back and forth,
the prayer-shawls around their shoulders. It was fun, she
thought, to be up in the gallery where the women were
seated, and look down upon the ceremonies that took place
below.

Finally the long-awaited moment came. The reading
of the weekly portion of the Pentateuch was concluded.
Then Danny was called up to read the Haftorah. Dressed
in the new suit, with the Talis around his shoulders,
Danny walked up to the reading desk before the altar, his
face shining with a sweet seriousness. How many times
he had rehearsed those now familiar Hebrew verses of the
Bible. A deep silence fell upon the congregation as the
clear young voice rose and fell in the chanting melody.
Simon looked up at Aunt Bess in the gallery. He saw her
lift her handkerchief to her eyes and wondered at it. How
could he know the thrill of pride and joy which filled her
heart at this moment. Her boy was formally entering into
the congregation of Israel and assuming the duties and
responsibilities of a man, under the Jewish law.

After the services, congratulations were showered upon
the happy family. Cake and wine were served to all the
people. Then a number of friends came directly from the

synagogue to Aunt Bess's home, where a fine dinner was served to them.

On Sunday afternoon a reception was held. Simon and Judy found it all very exciting and jolly. However, they did stop to think about the poor Jonathon children, who were home with the measles. Aunt Bess packed a special box of cookies and sent it to them.

THINGS TO DO AND TALK ABOUT
THE JEWISH HOME
BAR MITZVAH

Reviewing the Story

1. What daily ceremonies of Orthodox Jewish life are described in this story? Make a list of these before you discuss them.
2. Describe a Mezuzah and tell on what commandment of the Bible the custom of the Mezuzah is based. (See page 26)
3. What are the Jewish dietary laws? Make a list of these before you discuss them.

For Classroom Conversation

1. What do you think is the purpose of the Mezuzah?
2. Discuss some of the symbols used by people of other religions and the meanings these symbols have for them.
3. Discuss symbols used by some non-religious groups. Do you think symbols have any value?
4. What dietary laws do Catholics observe on certain days and during certain seasons?
5. Find out about dietary laws kept by other religious groups, such as the Mohammedans, Hindoos, and others. Perhaps certain members of the class could prepare reports on this subject.

Suggested Activities

1.

Each child might make a chart of the Jewish dietary laws. Plan your chart so that it will be interesting and different. Illustrate the chart with pictures.

2.

Draw a large picture illustrating one of the following scenes in the story:

1. Judy pointing to the Mezuzah on the doorpost and asking Uncle David what it is.
2. Danny putting on his new Tefilin and Talis, while grandfather and mother look on.
3. Danny in the synagogue, reading from the Torah on his Bar Mitzvah.
4. Danny showing Simon and Judy his Bar Mitzvah gifts.

PURIM

AS Simon walked down the hall past Ruthie's room, he heard a strange sound. Yes, someone was crying. Simon paused and listened for a moment to the stifled sobbing. Then, very quietly, he turned the knob of the door and peeped in. Ruthie was lying face downward on the bed, her shoulders shaking.

"Why, Ruthie," Simon was alarmed. "What's the matter? Aren't you well?" He sat down on the bed beside her and tried to get a glimpse of her face.

"Oh, it's nothing." Ruth sat up and smoothed back the tousled hair from her red eyes. "Mother would say it's just temper and I guess it is. Oh, Simon, I'm so *mad!*" She picked up the pillow and bounced it on the bed to relieve her feelings.

"Was it something that happened in religious school this morning?" Simon asked.

"Yes. For weeks I've been looking forward to being Queen Esther in the Purim play. Miss Miller, the leader of our dramatic club, had sort of led me to believe that I would get it. And then—this morning—" Ruthie's eyes filled with tears again, "she gave the part to Barbara Stein. And Barbara isn't as good as I am, really, Simon, she isn't. Only Miss Miller got mad at me last week because I asked her if she bleached her hair. And Barbara was so puffed-up about being Queen Esther, she would hardly talk to me."

"Gee!" Simon's tone was sympathetic. "I know how you feel. I sort of wanted to be Esther's uncle, Mordecai. But then, I couldn't because I had the main part in the Hanukah play last December. Still, I would have liked being in the Purim play, too."

"I guess the Jonathon family is being let down." Ruthie had to smile in spite of herself. "I know Maury wanted to be King Ahasuerus. He loves to strut around in royal robes and wave a scepter. But he got left out too."

"We ought to give our own Purim play," Simon remarked, and then suddenly he sat up so hard that the bed shook and Ruthie looked startled. "I have a grand idea. You remember what Uncle Phil was telling us last night about the way they used to celebrate Purim in the little village of Lithuania when he was a boy? There was a group of *Purim players* who went about from house to house and acted out the story of Purim. It was lots of fun, Uncle Phil said."

"You mean—" Ruthie began.

"Exactly," he interrupted her excitedly. "We can form our own band of Purim players and go around to the houses of our relatives and friends and give the play for them."

"Then I could be Queen Esther, after all." Ruth's face lighted up with joy.

"Of course. And I'll be Mordecai."

"Maury can be King Ahasuerus. Come on, let's tell him." The little girl grabbed Simon's hand and they dashed into the living room.

"A good idea," Maury nodded approvingly when the two burst out enthusiastically with the plan.

"I want to be in the Purim play too." Naomi screwed up her face, ready to cry.

"You can be my handmaiden," Ruthie agreed.

"Who'll be Haman?" Simon asked.

"We can get Bobby Feld, the boy next door," Maury suggested. "He belongs to the dramatic club at religious school and is pretty good."

"Dinner's ready," Aunt Elsa announced, appearing in the doorway. "What's all the excitement about?" she added. "But come, you'll tell me at the table."

Dr. and Mrs. Jonathon willingly gave their consent to the plan. "I'll help you with the costumes," Mrs. Jonathon agreed.

"Perhaps I can take a few hours off on Purim afternoon," Dr. Jonathon told them, "and drive you to the homes where you will give the play."

"To Aunt Bess's house first," Simon suggested.

"And then to Aunt Helen's," Ruthie put in.

"After that, to the rabbi's house," Maury said.

"Oh, it'll be such fun," Ruthie cried. "I'll ask Miss Miller for a copy of the Purim play that will be given in religious school. I know she'll let us use it."

For the next few weeks, the children were very busy learning their parts and working on costumes. Aunt Elsa said laughingly that she could take any of the parts herself after hearing the lines so often.

On the eve of Purim, the Jonathons and Simon went to a special service in the synagogue. The rabbi, in his beautiful, expressive voice, read the *Megillah,* as the "Book of Esther" is generally called.

On the day of Purim, right after school, the children got into their costumes amid much excitement. Dr. Jonathon, true to his word, was ready with the automobile.

When they reached the house where Aunt Bess lived, they knocked loudly on the door and cried, "Open to the Purim players!"

Aunt Bess was expecting them and had a houseful of guests to see the play. What fun it was! In the first scene, King Ahasuerus, ruler and conqueror of the mighty Persian empire, sat upon his throne in the great palace at the capital city, Shushan. Some time before, he had banished his beautiful wife, Vashti, from the throne because she had dared to disobey him. He had summoned her to appear one day when he and his guests were drinking and making merry. He wanted to show off her great beauty. But Vashti refused to come and she was therefore sent away from the palace in disgrace. And now the mighty monarch was choosing a new queen. Messengers had gone out to all parts of Persia, selecting the fairest maidens in the land from whom the king would make his choice. Beautifully dressed and perfumed, they all passed before the throne, to meet his royal inspection. Among the maidens was the beautiful young Jewess, Esther. She had been an orphan from early childhood and had been brought up by Mordecai, her uncle, who loved her as if she were his own daughter. Of all the lovely maidens, Esther was the most pleasing in the sight of the king and so he made her his queen instead of Vashti.

In the next scene, Mordecai, who frequently sat at the gate of the king's palace, overheard two guardsmen who plotted to harm the king because they were angry at him. Mordecai told Esther of the plot and she warned the king, telling him of Mordecai's act. The two plotters were hanged and the story was written down in the book of chronicles, where all the events of the empire were recorded.

In the third scene, appeared Haman, the proud and haughty prime minister of Persia, who expected that all should bow before him and do him honor. But Mordecai, the Jew, who sat at the palace gate, would not bow before Haman. For Mordecai would bow to no man—only to God. Then, in great rage and drunk with power, Haman vowed that he would be revenged, not only upon Mordecai, but upon all the Jews throughout the Persian empire.

As the play continued, Haman cunningly influenced the king to issue a decree ordering that all the Jews should be put to death on a certain day.

There was great mourning among the Jews. Mordecai was in despair. He told Esther that it was her duty to save her people. Perhaps it was for this very purpose that she had been raised to her high position. Esther sorrowfully reminded her uncle of the Persian law that no one dared to appear before the king without being summoned. Anyone who disobeyed this law was put to death unless the king held out his golden scepter, as a sign that the person's life was spared. And Esther told Mordecai that the king had not sent for her for the past thirty days.

But Esther was convinced by her uncle that she must have courage and appear before the king to plead for her people. She asked that first all the Jews in Shushan should fast for three days and three nights and pray for her.

The play went on. Esther, dressed in her most beautiful

gown, entered the great inner court, where the king sat. And he held out the golden scepter that was in his hand, for Esther found favor in his eyes. Then Esther drew near and touched the top of the scepter. And the king said, "What wilt thou, Queen Esther? For whatever thy request, even to the half of the kingdom, it shall be given thee."

And Esther said, "If it seem good unto the king, let the king and Haman come tomorrow to the banquet that I have prepared for him." The king agreed to do so.

That night, he could not sleep. He commanded that the book of chronicles should be read to him. When the story of how Mordecai had saved the king's life was read, Ahasuerus asked, "What honor and dignity hath been done to Mordecai for this?" He was told that nothing had been done. Then the king wanted to know what important official happened to be in the palace. Haman had just come in, for he wanted to ask the king for permission to hang Mordecai on the gallows which this wicked prime minister had prepared for him. When Haman entered, the king said to him, "What shall be done to the man whom the king delights to honor?"

Then Haman said to himself, "Whom would the king delight to honor besides myself?" And Haman said to the king, "For the man whom the king delights to honor, let royal robes be brought which the king used to wear, and the horse that the king rides upon, and a royal crown for his head. And let these be brought to one of the king's most noble princes, who will himself clothe the man whom the king delights to honor, and cause him to ride on horseback through the streets of the city and proclaim before him, 'Thus shall be done to the man whom the king delights to honor!'"

Then the king said to Haman, "Make haste, and take the robes and the horse, as thou hast said, and do even so to Mordecai, the Jew, that sits at the king's gate. Let nothing fail of all that thou hast spoken."

Then Haman carried out the commands of the king and led Mordecai on horseback through the streets, proclaiming, "Thus shall be done to the man whom the king delights to honor!"

The following scene showed Queen Esther entertaining King Ahasuerus and Haman at a banquet in her apartment. How proud Haman was at being honored in this way! The king was in a good mood and he said to his beautiful queen, "Whatever thy petition, it shall be granted thee, and whatever thy request, even to the half of the kingdom, it shall be performed."

Then Esther answered and said, "If I have found favor in thy sight, O king, and if it please the king, let my life be given me and my people, for we are to be destroyed."

Then Ahasuerus said to the queen, "Who is he and where is he that dares to do so?"

Then Esther replied, "An adversary and an enemy, even this wicked Haman." Then Haman was terrified before the king and queen and pleaded for his life. But Haman was hanged on the gallows which he had prepared for Mordecai, and the lives of the Jewish people were spared. And Mordecai was honored and made next in power to the king.

The play ended with the decree issued by Mordecai that the Jews were always to observe the day of their deliverance as a holiday of rejoicing and gladness, to be known as *Purim,* which means the *casting of lots.* For Haman had cast lots to decide the day on which the Jews were to be killed.

The guests applauded the play heartily, and the actors were treated to *Hamantaschen,* three-cornered cakes filled with poppy seeds and raisins. The shape was thought to resemble the hat worn by Haman.

The players didn't go to Aunt Helen's house because she had been present at Aunt Bess's home. Their next performance was at the home of the rabbi. There they gave the play in even better form. Then the weary actors were glad to return home and rest. But it had been fun, they all agreed.

Dinner, that evening, was a special holiday affair. When they were having their dessert, Ruthie suggested,

"Tell us some more about Purim when you were a boy.

You were interrupted the other night when you started—
remember? All we heard was about the Purim players
and then Mrs. Murphy had another one of her heart
attacks and you had to dash away."

"Purim was one of the happiest holidays of the year for
us," her father replied. "We looked forward to it for days.
On the eve of Purim, the synagogue was crowded for the
reading of the Megillah. We children were armed with
rattles made of wood and tin. Whenever the name of
Haman was mentioned, there was a great outburst of noise.
The rattles went into action, we shouted and stamped our
feet, expressing our disapproval of this wicked man. Some
of the older men became angry when the noise got too
loud and tried to quiet us. Most of the parents, however,
let us go on, for it was a custom of many years to let the
children drown out the hated name of Haman with loud
noise. Anyhow, this occasion was not really regarded as a
strictly religious service.

"As you know, Purim is not observed as a religious
holiday the way most of our other festivals are. After the
morning services, when the Megillah is read once more,
most people go about their usual tasks. But Purim has always been a beloved holiday. One of the customs we
youngsters loved most was *shalach-mones,* which means
the *sending of gifts.* These were usually good things to eat.
I had the privilege of carrying the shalach-mones to the

homes of our friends and relatives. As I walked along the
street, carefully carrying the covered dish, I would meet
my friends on the same errand, and we all felt very proud
and important. You can imagine, too, what a warm welcome the shalach-mones messenger received. My pockets
were stuffed with all sorts of goodies when I was through.

"I've already told you about the Purim players. They
went from house to house, acting out the story of Purim.
All the actors were men, even those who took the parts of
women. They usually made all the characters look and act
very comic. It was a gay sight to see them go singing
through the streets. Even the most serious and religious
Jews took part in the Purim antics. I remember one of
our most earnest Talmud students, who always dressed up
as Queen Esther and was the gayest actor of the troupe.
Never before did a queen walk with such a stride."

"In later years," Uncle Phil continued, "when I was a
student in the Yeshiva, which is a Talmudical college,
Purim was celebrated merrily there too. Most of the time,
you see, we were all very serious about our studies. On
Purim, very little studying went on. We held a sort of all-
day carnival. We chose one of the students to act as a
Purim-rabbi. He could say anything he liked and could
even make jokes about the head rabbi of the Yeshiva. The
Purim-rabbi usually preached a sermon giving humorous
explanations about certain points in the Talmud, and tell-

ing funny stories. Of course, we always chose a rather clever fellow to be the Purim-rabbi."

"It certainly sounds jolly," Maury cried. "I think we should choose a Purim-rabbi in religious school."

"Purim really began in Persia, didn't it?" Aunt Elsa asked. "Because that's where the Purim story took place."

"That's right," Uncle Phil agreed. "And that reminds me of some interesting things I read recently telling how the Jews of Persia celebrate Purim."

"You mean nowadays?" asked Simon.

"Yes," his uncle replied. "Don't forget that there are Jews in Persia today as well as in the days of the Bible. Naturally, Purim is a specially important festival for them.

"On Purim eve, the Megillah is read, of course. Every time the name of Haman is mentioned, the children not only make a great deal of noise, but also shoot off fireworks. Later in the evening, they put on masquerade costumes and go from house to house, singing and dancing.

"On Purim morning, the children usually receive a gift of money from their parents. The most important event of the morning is the burning of the effigy of Haman. This is a huge stuffed figure filled with straw and rags, which the children had prepared in advance. It is hung from a pole, and set on fire. The children stand around watching it, clapping their hands, and calling, 'Haman, the wicked, Haman, the wicked.' "

"Dr. Jonathan," the maid interrupted suddenly, after answering the phone, "there is an emergency call for you. Please come right away."

"I'll tell you more later," the doctor promised as he hurried away.

About an hour later, when Dr. Jonathon returned, he had a pleasant-looking young man with him, whom the children had never met before. "This is Dr. Ben Joseph," their father told him. "He is going to be my new assistant in the office. Dr. Ben Joseph is from Palestine and I know he will be able to tell you many interesting things about that country."

"And they will be able to tell me much more about this country, I am sure," the young doctor replied. "So when I return to Palestine, I will be able to tell the children there about this wonderful United States."

"Do you celebrate Purim in Palestine?" asked Ruthie, looking up at him with her friendly smile.

"Indeed we do," he assured her. "It is one of our most delightful holidays."

"Please tell us," the children cried.

"I warned you," Dr. Jonathon laughed as he looked at the younger man. "The favorite expression around here is 'Tell us.'"

"I will be delighted," Dr. Ben Joseph said. "I am always happy to talk about Palestine."

"First, you must have a cup of tea and some Haman-taschen," Aunt Elsa insisted.

"I lived in Jerusalem," Dr. Ben Joseph began as he sat at the table and drank his tea. "But I always went to the city of Tel Aviv to celebrate Purim. Many people do this and Tel Aviv is always crowded with visitors on this holiday. For although Purim is celebrated all over Palestine, the gayest and most interesting events take place in Tel Aviv.

"Now, let us imagine that you are all there with me. It is the eve of Purim. The streets are crowded with people. Everyone is in a gay, holiday mood. Many of the children are already in masquerade costumes, wearing false faces of all kinds. In fact, they begin to wear these costumes several days before Purim. Suddenly we hear bells ring-ing and the shrill blowing of horns. Purim has begun. Let us follow the large crowds to the open space in front of the Opera House. In the distance, we see the sun moving westward, ready for its drop into the Mediterranean Sea. The streets are now filled with a slowly-moving mass of people. In front of the Opera House, a band is playing. We are attracted by a large platform which is built out-side the third floor windows of the Opera House. There, a scene from the story of Purim is portrayed, with large figures dressed in bright-colored costumes. We see Queen Esther entertaining King Ahasuerus and Haman. It looks very gay and can be seen from a long distance.

"The band plays a number of lively tunes. Everyone greets each other with 'Good Purim, Good Purim.' The mayor makes a speech.

"After awhile, the crowds grow smaller. Dusk begins to fall. Many of the people are going to the synagogues to hear the reading of the Megillah. Let us go, too. We approach the Great Synagogue, the largest of Tel Aviv. It has a beautiful dome which can be seen above many of the housetops. The synagogue is filled with a large gathering. We listen as the rabbi reads the scroll of the *Book of Esther*. Many of the people in the congregation understand every word of the beautiful biblical Hebrew, for Hebrew is the everyday language of Palestine.

"After the services, we go back to our hotel, where a special Purim meal is served to us. Soon after, we find ourselves on the streets again, for the Purim carnival is now on. We are especially delighted with the Street of the Sea, a long avenue on the edge of the beach, where people sit at open cafes or on the porches of hotels and enjoy the breezes from the sea. All Tel Aviv is celebrating. Many people are in gay masquerade costumes and go through the streets singing and making noise with rattles and horns."

"It sounds like a combination of New Year's Eve and Halloween, here in the United States," said Maury.

"Later in the evening," Dr. Ben Joseph continued, "par-

ties and balls are held both in public buildings and in private homes. The carnival in the streets lasts most of the night. We look in at the Opera House, where a masquerade party is in progress. Dancing is going on. Everyone seems to be having a good time.

"The next day, which is Purim, the merry-making goes on. The children wear their costumes all day long. The big event of the afternoon is the annual Purim parade. Many organizations take part in it, such as schools, clubs, agricultural settlements, labor groups, industries, and so forth. We are lucky to find room on the upper balcony of our hotel, which happens to be on the street where the parade is passing.

"The sidewalks are filled with people. The balconies of other buildings are crowded with guests. We find the parade very interesting and colorful. There are floats of all kinds, showing the work of the pioneers in Palestine and the progress they are making. There are also biblical scenes. At the head of the parade rides the fair Queen Esther, who won this honor by being voted the most beautiful girl.

"But it is impossible to describe all the colorful scenes that make up this Purim parade."

"It certainly sounds very interesting," Dr. Jonathon declared. "I'd like to see it some day."

On the following Sunday, the Purim play was to be

given at the Synagogue School. As Ruthie's class filed into the assembly room, the little girl was eager to see how Barbara would play the part of Queen Esther. Disappointment and anger had long since vanished from her heart.

The whole school was assembled. There were many visitors. It was time for the curtain to go up. Minutes passed. The children became restless, and the grown-ups wondered why the play did not begin.

Then the curtains parted and the familiar figure of the rabbi appeared. "My dear children," he began, "and our good friends who have come to see the Purim play. I regret to tell you that a most unfortunate thing has just happened. The little girl who was to play the part of Queen Esther has met with an accident. She tripped over her long gown and fell down the stairs leading to the wing of the stage. Barbara is not badly hurt but she sprained her ankle and will not be able to play the part. And we can hardly get another Queen Esther at this late hour."

A murmur of disappointment swept over the audience. To be deprived of their Purim play at the last moment seemed too much.

Suddenly the rabbi's eye fell upon Ruthie, who was sitting in the first row.

"Wait a minute," he cried. "I think we have a Queen Esther. Ruth Jonathon, you played the part beautifully in my own home, a few days ago. Will you help us out now?"

And so Ruthie became, not only Queen Esther, the heroine of the Jewish people, but also the heroine of the school.

After the play, Ruthie insisted on bringing to Barbara the beautiful bouquet of flowers that was handed to her at the end of the play.

THINGS TO DO AND TALK ABOUT
PURIM

Reviewing the Story

Tell which characters in the Purim story said each of the following, to whom they were speaking, and under what circumstances the speech was made:

1. "There is a certain people scattered throughout thy kingdom and their laws are different from those of other people. If it please the king, let it be written that they be destroyed."
2. "Who knows whether it was not for this very purpose that you were raised to this high position."
3. "Think not that thou shalt escape in the king's house more than all the Jews."
4. "I will go unto the king, which is not according to the law; and if I perish, I perish."
5. "Whatever thy request, even to the half of my kingdom, it shall be granted."
6. "What honor and dignity hath been done to Mordecai for this?"
7. "Thus shall be done to the man whom the king delights to honor."
8. "Let my life be given me at my petition, and my people at my request."
9. "Who is he and where is he that dares to do so?"
10. "Hang him thereon."

For Classroom Conversation

1. Tell some of the interesting Purim customs observed by the Jews of Persia.
2. Describe a Purim celebration in Tel Aviv.
3. What was the most interesting Purim celebration in which you have ever taken part?
4. Why do you think Purim is such a beloved holiday to the Jewish people?
5. How does the story of Purim bring courage to the Jewish people in present times?

Suggested Activities

1.

Making a Class Megillah—Make a class Megillah of the *Book of Esther*. It should be in the form of a scroll when completed. Work in groups if you like. Each group should decide which part of the story it will take. The story may be written in your own words but should follow the biblical style as much as possible. Quote freely from the Bible in the conversational parts of the story.

Use a thin but strong bond paper. Write the story in printed letters. Paste the pages together to form a long strip, so you can roll it in the form of a scroll. Illustrate your story with pen and ink drawings. Use ink of various colors, if you like.

Attach the scroll to rollers. Decorate the rollers at the top and bottom.

2.

Organize one or more groups of Purim players. Either make up your own play about the Purim story or get a printed play.

Rehearse the play. Present it in other classrooms or at the homes of friends.

3.

The Purim story is very suitable for a puppet show, marionette show, or shadow play.[1]

[1] Note to Teacher: For general directions on how to present shows like these, see *Pupil's Activity Book, Volume Two,* by Dorothy F. Zeligs.

PASSOVER

"THERE, don't you think I did a pretty good job?" Ruthie stepped back, cloth in hand, to admire the pair of silver candlesticks which she had polished until they sparkled.

"But why are you doing that?" asked Simon. "We're going to grandfather's house for the Seder."

"Yes, I know," she replied. "But on a holiday I want the candlesticks to be looking their best, whether they're on *active duty* or not.

"What's the matter, Simon?" she continued, as her cousin made no further response but continued to lean against the kitchen wall, his hands in his pockets and a forlorn look in his brown eyes.

"Oh, nothing—yes, those candlesticks sure look fine, Ruth."

"Come on, Si, tell me about it," Ruthie coaxed in a soft voice. "I always tell you things."

"It isn't anything really important—I'm just sort of disappointed, that's all. You know, I've been saving up my allowance for three months so that I could buy a pair of roller skates."

"Oh, Simon, did something happen to that money?" Ruth's tone was full of concern. "Why, you've been talking about those skates for weeks."

"I lost it yesterday," the boy confessed unhappily. "Aunt Elsa kept warning me not to carry the money around with me all the time, but I thought it was fun to open my folding-bill and see the dollar bills. On the way home, yesterday, I stopped at a corner where a crowd had gathered to watch a man who was advertising hair tonic. And when I got home, my purse was gone."

"Did you tell mother and daddy?" Ruth asked.

"Yes," Simon nodded, "and I got a scolding too."

"I'm terribly sorry." Ruth's blue eyes were sympathetic. Then, suddenly, she brightened up and gave a cry of delight. "I know how you can get your skates, Simon— on the night of the Seder."

"What in the world do you mean?" He stared at her unbelievingly.

"Well, you see," Ruthie explained, "anyone who hides the Afikomon and keeps it till the end of the Seder gets any gift he asks for."

"What's the Af—what did you call it?"

"Why, you learned about it in religious school the other day," the little girl reminded him reproachfully. "The

Afikomon is a piece of matzo. It represents the lamb which the Hebrews sacrificed just before they departed from Egypt. Daddy wraps this matzo in a napkin and puts it aside. The Seder can't be ended properly without each one eating a piece of the Afikomon, so the child who manages to slip it away and hide it can demand a gift for its return. I'll help you get it and then you can ask daddy for a pair of skates."

"What fun! Gee, Ruthie, you're a real pal." Simon's gloom had vanished completely. "You know, this is going to be my very first Seder. We never used to have any at home."

"We'll have to watch so that Maury or Cousin Danny don't get it," Ruth reminded him. "Maury is planning to ask daddy for a candid camera. But he has a birthday next month, so he can wait. Anyhow, he has a whole roomful of pictures already."

The approaching holiday was making itself felt in the Jonathon home. The spring cleaning was being completed. There was a smell of fresh paint in the air. New curtains were hung on all the windows. The whole apartment had a pleasant freshness and sparkle about it, seeming to say that it was all ready for Passover.

Then there was the important matter of getting new spring clothes to be worn on the holiday. There were busy shopping days for everyone, and great excitement when the new suits, dresses, hats, and shoes were delivered to the door.

Simon had been looking forward to his first Seder for weeks. He and the Jonathons were going to Aunt Bess and Uncle David's home, where grandfather would conduct the Seder.

When the day finally arrived, it was delightfully warm and spring-like. The trip to the suburb where their relatives lived was a pleasant one. Aunt Bess looked a bit flushed and flurried when she met them at the door, but her welcome had its usual hearty ring.

Around sunset, the men went to the synagogue for services. When they returned, the family gathered around the festive table. "It looks very lovely," Dr. Jonathon said appreciatively. In the center stood a vase of delicately colored spring flowers. On either side were the silver candlesticks in which burned the holiday candles. The lovely dishes, the shining glassware, the polished silver, all looked very attractive on the fine linen cloth. At the head of the table there was a large Passover platter decorated with interesting pictures about the holiday. It contained the Seder symbols—the roasted shankbone of lamb, a roasted egg, some bitter herbs in the form of horse-radish, parsley, and *haroses,* which was a mixture of apples, almonds, and raisins, finely chopped and flavored with cinnamon and wine. On another plate were three matzos covered with

an embroidered Passover cloth. In front of each place stood a wine goblet. Grandfather's was a large one made of silver, but the others were of fine crystal. The children's glasses were now filled with grape juice, while the grown-ups had wine.

"Each one must have a *Haggadah* in which to follow the Seder service," Dr. Jonathon said, passing out attractive little books which were beautifully illustrated. The word *Haggadah* means story. The *Haggadah* contains the story of Passover as it is told in the Seder service. "Now, grandfather," Dr. Jonathon continued, "I think we are ready to begin."

Grandfather, dressed in a new suit, his white hair and beard trim and shining, was feeling very happy. He raised his silver goblet and in a deep, expressive voice chanted the blessing over the wine. The Seder had begun.

"It's good," declared Naomi, emptying her glass with one long gulp. Everybody laughed, and Naomi looked very pleased with herself.

At a signal from her mother, Ruthie now got up and brought to grandfather's side a small silver basin and pitcher for the ceremonial hand-washing. He poured some water over his hands, dried them on a linen towel which hung over Ruthie's arm, and smiled at her. Then he took a piece of parsley and dipped it in salt-water. Each one followed grandfather's example as the plate of parsley was passed around, and then they recited the prayer together, first in Hebrew and then in English. "Blessed art Thou, O Lord our God, King of the Universe, Creator of the fruits of the earth."

Grandfather now took the middle matzo from a plate which held three of them. He broke it in half and wrapped one part in a large napkin. Ruthie and Simon exchanged significant glances. This was to be the Afikomon. Then he lifted the dish containing the matzos and recited, " 'Lo, this is the bread of affliction which our ancestors ate in the land of Egypt. Let all who are hungry come and eat. Let all who are in need come and celebrate the Passover with us. May it be God's will to redeem us from all trouble and all slavery. Next year at this season, may the whole house of Israel be free.' "

"And now," grandfather paused expectantly, "we are ready for the *Questions*."

"Oh, that's fine," cried Simon, "because there are about a dozen buzzing around in my head." A shout of laughter greeted this innocent remark and poor Simon's face turned a deep red.

"Naomi gets to ask the *Four Questions*," Maury said importantly. "She's the youngest." He had taught her the questions and was eager to show off his little pupil.

"Later on, you may ask as many as you like," Uncle Phil said comfortingly to his nephew and Simon recovered quickly from his embarrassment.

"That's right," grandfather agreed. "The word *Seder* means *order of service* and so we shall follow the services in their regular order."

Naomi was happy to be the center of attention. She recited the *Four Questions* in Hebrew very nicely, translating each one into English. She asked to be informed why this night was different from all other nights, and what the various ceremonies and symbols meant.

"The whole Seder is the answer to your questions," grandfather replied, "and its purpose is to explain the story of Passover to you."

"Perhaps I should tell you first," Dr. Jonathon said, "that Passover has two meanings. Chiefly, it is the great festival of freedom, celebrating the release of the Children of Israel from their slavery in Egypt. However, it is also a festival of the spring harvest. It recalls to our minds the time when our ancestors lived in Palestine in ancient days, and celebrated the gathering of the spring crop of grain at this season."

As the Seder proceeded, the children learned the meaning of the Seder symbols and ceremonies. The tender green parsley represented the spring and the new life which this season brought to the earth. It was dipped in salt-water to remind the Jews of the tears which their ancestors shed as they labored in the service of their oppressors in Egypt. The haroses, with its reddish color, was a reminder of the mortar and brick with which the Hebrews had been forced to work. The meaning of the roasted shankbone was the most interesting of all, Simon thought. It was a symbol of the *Pesach* or *paschal* lamb which the Israelites ate at their last meal in Egypt, on the eve before their departure. Dr. Jonathon explained how the Israelites had been instructed by Moses to gather in front of their homes, at dusk. The head of each family took a lamb and offered it as a sacrifice to God. The lamb was then roasted whole over a bonfire, and eaten together with bitter herbs and unleavened bread. By sacrificing the lamb, the Jews showed their faith in God and their disbelief in the Egyptian gods, for the lamb was a sacred animal in Egypt. The Bible tells us that during this night, the first-born of all the Egyptians died. Then Pharaoh, in fear and trembling, bade the Hebrews go.

Later on, when the Jews were living in Palestine, they offered sacrifices in the Temple in memory of the paschal lamb. Of these, also, the roasted shankbone on the Seder plate remind us. The roasted egg stands for the usual sacrifices that were once made in the Temple at Jerusalem on a number of holidays.

What about the matzos? We are told that the Hebrews

had to leave Egypt in such a hurry that they could not even wait for the dough of their bread to rise. So they took it with them and baked it unleavened in the desert. Besides, their kneading-troughs had already been packed up in the clothes which they carried upon their shoulders. The *Haggadah* calls matzos the *bread of affliction*. Perhaps this is because the Hebrews probably had to eat their bread unleavened many times even while they were in Egypt, in the days of their slavery, when they had little time to prepare their food. In the countries of the East, poor people today still eat unleavened bread most of the time. But matzo has become the symbol of the *bread of freedom,* for our ancestors ate it as free men, after their escape from Egypt.

"Many people consider Passover the greatest of the Jewish holidays," Dr. Jonathon told the children. "It is the anniversary of our freedom. Because our ancestors had the courage to free themselves, and because they had the wonderful leadership of a man like Moses, the Jews were transformed from an enslaved people into a nation which contributed much to the civilization of the world.

"We Jews must always be on the side of human freedom," he continued. "That is the message of Passover. In our Seder service we say, 'And a stranger thou shalt not wrong, neither shalt thou oppress him; for ye were strangers in the land of Egypt.' "

By the time the Seder meal was served, Naomi's head

was drooping lower and lower. She woke up long enough to have something to eat and then Aunt Elsa put her to bed.

Simon had forgotten all about the Afikomon. But Ruthie, who was helping to serve the dinner, slipped something into his hand, under the table, and moved quickly away. It was the half matzo wrapped in a napkin. Simon almost laughed out loud, for at that very moment he saw Maury grope suddenly behind his back for the missing treasure and then cast a look of mingled admiration and disgust at the innocent face of his sister.

When the meal was over, grandfather reached for the Afikomon. He pretended to be very much disturbed when he found that it was missing. "We must have it," he declared. "The Seder meal cannot be finished properly without it. For this piece of matzo is a symbol of the paschal lamb. In ancient times, each person at the Seder received a small portion of the paschal lamb for dessert. In memory of this we eat the Afikomon at the end of the Seder meal."

"Would it be worth a pair of skates to you?" Simon asked.

"Well—" Grandfather pretended to be doubtful. "What do you think, Uncle Phil?"

"I don't see how we can escape it," Uncle Phil replied in a serious tone. And that was how Simon got a pair of skates with which to remember his first Seder.

But the Seder wasn't over with the serving of dinner, Simon discovered. The second part was very jolly. He was especially interested in the ceremony of opening the door for the prophet Elijah. There is a legend that this ancient prophet visits every Jewish home on Seder night and partakes of the wine that is poured for him in the special cup known as the *Cup of Elijah*. There is an old belief that Elijah will return some day and lead all the Jewish people back to Palestine. His coming, it is said, will bring a new era of peace and happiness to the whole world. On Passover, when Jews are celebrating their freedom from slavery, it seems a suitable time to think of the ancient prophet who has become a symbol of freedom and emancipation.

So now, as Ruthie got up and held open the door, she looked out a little breathlessly. That rustle of wind—was it the movement of some invisible presence that passed her? The other children peered eagerly into the large silver goblet standing on the table. Were they imagining it, or did the wine really get less as the unseen Elijah sipped from it?

The Seder continued with the delightful songs and hymns found in the *Haggadah*. One person would lead and the rest would join in the refrain. One of the merriest songs was *An Only Kid*. The children's voices grew louder with each stanza.

"Then came the dog
And bit the cat
That ate the kid
My father bought
For two *zuzim*.
An only kid!
An only kid!"

When the Seder was finally over, Simon suddenly found that he was quite tired and sleepy. No wonder! It was hours past his usual bedtime.

Passover was a delightfully long holiday, lasting eight days, Simon learned. It was fun having matzos instead of bread at every meal.

One evening during the week of Passover, the Jonathon family was gathered in the living room. Simon was delighted to find that everyone was going to be at home. Now he would get Uncle Phil to tell about Pesach in the small village of Lithuania, when he was a boy. Simon entered into a rapid conspiracy with his cousins and soon the unsuspecting Dr. Jonathon found the evening paper being gently removed from his hands.

"Tell us about Pesach when you were a boy," Ruthie said coaxingly as she sat down on the arm of his chair.

Dr. Jonathon laughed and pulled her hair. His wife, sitting in a chair opposite him, put down her paper too. She loved to hear him talk about his boyhood days just as much as the children did.

"Pesach was one of the most exciting holidays of the year," Uncle Phil began promptly. He seldom needed coaxing to talk on his favorite subject. "As soon as Purim was over, plans for Pesach were being discussed. It was the holiday for which we boys got our yearly suit of clothes and our yearly pair of shoes. So we went with our mothers to visit the tailor and the shoe-maker. 'He grows fast,' my mother would say, looking at me proudly, 'so be sure to make the suit extra large, for a whole year's growth.' Most of the children generally wore clothes that were too big, because it took us almost a whole year to catch up with the space that had been allowed for growing. Except," he added, "when we wore things handed down from an older brother or sister. Then our clothes were usually too small and we would stick out at the wrists and ankles.

"When it was time to begin baking the matzos, we felt that Pesach was really close at hand. There were several bakers in the village. They had large ovens and baked the matzos for everyone. Each family would provide its own flour and pay the baker for doing the work. The rabbi would supervise carefully to see that everything was *kosher for Passover*.

"We always went along with father and mother to bring our matzos home. These were carried on a clean white sheet, each of the four corners held by a different person. It was like a sort of jolly parade, carrying those matzos home.

"For the poor people, matzos were provided through a special fund. Practically everyone contributed to this fund except those who had to receive its benefits.

"The coming of Pesach meant the coming of spring. We boys rejoiced that the long cold winter was over and the heavy snows were melting. Some of us dared to go barefoot for the first time. It was good to feel the mud oozing between our toes.

"In each little cottage a thorough house-cleaning was going on. Everything must be made clean and shining for Passover. The walls were whitewashed, floors were scrubbed, every nook and corner of the house was made clean and fresh.

"These days before Pesach were busy ones for our mothers and sisters, but we lads of the Heder loved them. For almost two weeks before Pesach, we had school for only half a day instead of a full day. We studied the *Haggadah* and our teacher told us many stories in connection with it.

"On the night before Pesach, I always helped my father in the ceremony of *searching for leaven*."

"What's that?" asked Simon.

"Leaven or *hometz* is any foodstuff that is not kosher for Passover use. You know that the difference between bread and matzo is that bread contains yeast, which causes the dough to rise. Matzo is flat and hard because it has no yeast. Another word for yeast is *leaven*. Anything that contains leaven is unfit for Passover. In order to be sure that the home is all ready for the holiday, the master of the house searches carefully in all nooks and corners for any remaining leaven. Of course, there isn't any in a house that has been so thoroughly cleaned, so something must

be done about it. The ceremony of *searching for leaven* and reciting the proper prayer has to be carried out. Mother, therefore, placed bits of bread in various parts of the house.

"It was fun to go with father searching for leaven. He carried an old wooden spoon in one hand and a few goose feathers in the other. I would hold a candle to light the way. Mother went ahead and showed him where she had put the *hometz*. As father swept the bits of bread into the spoon with the feathers, he recited the prayer for this occasion. Then he wrapped the spoon and its contents in a piece of paper and tied it with cord. This *hometz* was burned in a big oven at the synagogue the next morning. The sexton came through the streets calling, 'Burn your hometz,' and all the men would come out of their homes to obey. After that ceremony, everyone had to be careful not to scatter any crumbs in the house, for everything was ready for Pesach.

"The next morning, the last meal at which bread could be eaten was served. Then the few remaining dishes that had not yet been packed away were gathered up and hidden. The Passover dishes had been unpacked and washed. Pots and pans had been scoured and heated to make them kosher for Pesach. The silverware had been made ready too. They had been thoroughly polished and then dipped into boiling hot water. It used to be my job to tie each

knife, fork, and spoon on a long cord, separating each by
a knot with about an inch of cord between. Then father
would dip the whole thing into a pot of boiling water. He
would keep it there a short time and then draw it out
again by the edge of the cord.

"What baking and cooking and stewing there went on
this final day. For at sunset, the long-awaited eight-day
festival would begin and the first Seder would be held.

"It was my duty to go to the home of a certain Jew who
prepared the haroses for every family. We each gave a
small donation for this and the money was used for charity.

"When evening came, everything was ready for the
Seder. The house was spotless and shining. We were
dressed in our new clothes. The table was set with Passover dishes, and from the kitchen came delicious odors of
good food.

"The hurry and flurry of weeks of preparation was over.
There was a look of peace and happiness on mother's face
as she lit the festival candles on the table and recited the
blessing.

"Father and I went to the synagogue for the short evening services. When we returned home, we flung open the
door and cried, 'Good Yom Tov, Good Yom Tov.' Then
the Seder began. Father's explanations about the *Haggadah* were so interesting and he had so many stories from
the Talmud to tell about each point that mother would

despair of ever getting through. She would declare that
the matzo-meal balls would be hard as iron from standing so long.

"After the meal came the jolliest part of the Seder—the
songs and hymns which we would all chant together."

"Did you ever find the Afikomon which your father
hid?" asked Ruthie.

"Indeed I did," he assured her.

"The whole festival of Pesach was delightful," he went
on. "We boys would gather in each other's homes or in
the synagogue courtyard, or on the streets, and play games
with our nuts. We enjoyed the good holiday meals and
the freedom from school. Yes," concluded Dr. Jonathon,
"those were great days—happy days."

THINGS TO DO AND TALK ABOUT

PASSOVER

Reviewing the Story

1. What two meanings does the holiday of Passover have for the Jewish people?
2. Tell the meaning of the following symbols used at the Seder: haroses; the shankbone; bitter herbs; the egg; matzos.
3. What does the word *Seder* mean? What is the *Haggadah*? Who generally asks the *Four Questions*? What is the Afikomon and what interesting custom is connected with it?
4. What interesting things did Uncle Phil remember about the Passover season when he was a boy?

For Classroom Conversation

1. Which of the customs described in the story are kept in your home? Which ones are not?
2. Do you think Passover meant more to Uncle Phil as a boy than it does to you? Discuss.
3. The events of the first Passover took place more than three thousand years ago. Has the ideal for which the ancient Hebrews struggled then been achieved in the world yet? Discuss.
4. What great qualities of leadership did Moses possess which enabled him to accomplish his great task successfully?
5. Tell about other groups of people or nations who, at various times in their history, fought for the ideal of human freedom.

171

6. Tell about some pleasant Passover experiences which you enjoyed in your home.

Suggested Activities

1.

Prepare a Seder service, either for your own class or to be presented at a school assembly. Perhaps the whole school could take part in a Seder service together. Learn the ceremonies, prayers, stories, and songs needed for the Seder.

2.

Make covers for the Haggadahs which you use at the Seder.

3.

Paint large pictures about the Passover story and use them to decorate the room in which you hold the Seder.

4.

Make a Seder plate, either out of paper or clay. Paint on it pictures about Passover.

SHOVUOS

SIMON'S class at the Synagogue School was a very busy place about a week before Shovuos. Groups of children in various parts of the room were putting the finishing touches on the dioramas which they were making about the coming holiday. On the following Sunday, the class was going to show its work to the school, at the weekly assembly.

Simon was quite thrilled with the clay figure of Moses, which he had just completed. As he placed it in the diorama, on the slope of Mt. Sinai, several children watched.

"It's wonderful, Simon," cried one boy.

"I bet you'll be a sculptor when you grow up," said another. Simon was happy as he heard their praise. He had worked very hard at his difficult task. The background of the diorama was a circular-shaped painting showing a desert scene. Sand and rocks and a few stunted bushes here and there gave a good picture of the desert of Sinai. At one end of the small stage stood Mt. Sinai. Many clay figures dressed in colorful costumes were gathered at the foot of the mountain. They were the Children of Israel, looking up at their leader Moses. Above the diorama there was a large clay model of the Tablets of the Law, with the number of each commandment printed on it in Hebrew.

"We're ready to begin our rehearsal," said the chairman of the group. "You start, Nathan."

Nathan cleared his throat and fingered his paper a bit nervously. "This diorama," he said, "shows the Israelites gathered at the foot of Mt. Sinai. A great event is taking place. The Children of Israel are receiving the Ten Commandments, which they will pass on to the whole civilized world. The Bible gives a very exciting description of this scene. There was a great storm on Mt. Sinai. Clouds covered the top of the mountain and there were blinding flashes of lightning and loud bursts of thunder. Blasts of the shofar were heard. The whole earth seemed to shake. The people waited in trembling silence, for it was a thrilling and fearful moment. Then they heard a voice saying, 'I am the Lord, thy God, who brought thee out of the land of Egypt, out of the house of bondage. Thou shalt have no other gods before Me.' And when the people had heard all the commandments, they replied, 'All that the Lord hath spoken we will do.'

"Thus, our ancestors accepted the commandments of God and promised to obey them. For this reason, Shovuos really marks the birthday of the Jews as a religious people.

In those ancient days, all the nations around them were worshiping idols. In the land of Egypt, where the Jews had been slaves for many years, they saw idols being worshiped. The desert tribes around them had many gods. Only the Jews believed in one God. And now, at Mt. Sinai, they promised to worship the one true God and to obey His commandments for all time."

When his group had finished the rehearsal, Simon went over to hear Maury, who was just saying his part in another group. The diorama made by this group was very interesting, Simon thought. It showed a harvest scene in Palestine among the ancient Hebrews at the Shovuos season. It was the time of the ripening of the wheat.

"Shovuos," Maury was saying, "has another meaning besides the one you have just heard. It is also a harvest festival of thanksgiving, for at this season, our ancestors, who were farmers in Palestine, gathered in the new crop of wheat. So, Shovuos, like Passover, not only celebrates a historic event, but also reminds us of the agricultural life which the Jews once led in Palestine.

"Our scene shows the farmers of ancient Palestine working in the fields. We see the men dressed in short tunics reaching to their knees, with girdles tied around their waists. The women wore longer garments of the same kind. Their clothes were of bright colors, blue, green, or red. These must have made the harvest fields look very

gay. We have shown you here the different tasks that were necessary to harvest the grain. Some of the people are cutting the wheat with their scythes. Others are binding the grain into sheaves. At this end of the diorama we see threshing going on. A farmer is driving a heavy sledge drawn by oxen, over the piles of grain. Rough stones have been hammered into the bottom of the sledge and these tear the chaff from the kernels. Near the front of the scene, there are several women winnowing. They toss the grain up into the air in a large sieve. The wind catches the light chaff and blows it away, while the grain remains."

Simon thought that Maury's group had worked out the diorama very cleverly. They had used real sheaves of wheat and wheat kernels. The people were made of cardboard and painted. The oxen were small toy animals. The painted background showed more fields and the blue, clear sky of Palestine.

In another diorama, Simon saw the Hebrew farmers of ancient Palestine bringing the offerings of their first fruits to the Temple in Jerusalem, just as they used to do on Shovuos. The baskets which they carried on their heads contained grapes, figs, and pomegranates, barley, and wheat. Some of them had large jugs filled with olive-oil or honey, balanced on their shoulders. It was a gay procession, Simon learned from the speaker who described the scene. The pilgrims sang and played on musical instruments as they marched to the Temple with their offerings.

A fourth diorama showed the inner courtyard of the Temple and the priests preparing for the Shovuos services. One of them was holding the two loaves of bread baked from the new crop of grain, which were offered as a special sacrifice on this festival.

"The word *Shovuos,*" a little girl was explaining, "means *weeks* in Hebrew, and this holiday is also known as the *Feast of Weeks,* for Shovuos comes exactly seven weeks after Passover, on the fiftieth day. These seven weeks are the period of the grain harvest in Palestine, which begins with the barley crop at Passover and ends with the wheat crop at Shovuos. So you see," she concluded, "Shovuos has two meanings for us. It shows us that the Jews are both the people of the Book and the people of the Plow."

A fifth diorama showed a Shovuos scene in modern Palestine. A procession of Jewish farmers were carrying their first fruits as offerings, just as our ancestors used to do. But instead of bringing them to the Temple, they brought them to certain centers throughout the country. There, special ceremonies were held and the offerings were given to the Jewish National Fund. The money received for these gifts was used by the Fund to buy more land in Palestine for the Jewish people. Thus, the old ceremony of ancient times was brought to life once more.

As Simon was returning to his seat, the telephone in the classroom rang. A sudden quiet descended as the teacher lifted the receiver from the hook. "Yes, he's here. I'll send him right down.

"Simon," he turned to the surprised youngster. "The rabbi wants to see you in his study."

With mingled feelings of excitement and uneasiness, Simon started for the door while his classmates stared at him curiously. From the other side of the room, Maury smiled at him encouragingly. It was no small matter to be summoned to the rabbi's study, Simon knew. His heart was beating somewhat rapidly as he stood before the huge, paneled door and knocked timidly. No reply. He knocked more loudly.

"Come in," called a hearty voice, and Simon found himself facing the pleasant, kindly rabbi, who greeted him with a friendly smile. "Sit down, Simon," he waved the boy towards a chair. "I have a surprise for you," he continued, after a moment. "How would you like to be confirmed this Shovuos—together with your cousin Maurice?"

"Oh," Simon caught his breath at the thought. "Oh, Rabbi Golding, could I really?"

The rabbi smiled at his eagerness. "Yes, you could," he replied. "At the last teachers' meeting, it was suggested that you should be considered a member of the Confirmation class. I was told that you have made unusual progress in your work this year. You have come to us from a small town, with practically no Jewish background. Yet you have shown a fine interest in acquiring Jewish knowledge and have done a great deal of extra reading in addition to your regular classroom work. Moreover, you have attended my Confirmation class faithfully, although you were not a regular member."

"I came with Maury because I liked it," Simon said slowly, still somewhat overcome. "But I didn't think—"

"Yes, I know," Rabbi Golding replied. "That is why we consider you ready for Confirmation. You have shown a genuine interest in your studies apart from any thought of reward. Very well, my boy." The rabbi shook Simon's hand and walked to the door with him.

Simon's feet hardly touched the pavement as he and Maury flew home, with Ruth and Naomi struggling to keep up. "Wait for me, Maury," called Naomi.

"Oh, Simon, I'm so thrilled about your being confirmed," Ruthie cried breathlessly.

"It's great," put in Maury enthusiastically. "Now we'll be able to have a double reception and do everything together. It's almost like being twins. But hurry, we must tell mother and daddy about it."

The Jonathon dinner table was the center of much excited discussion that day. Aunt Elsa and Uncle Phil were delighted with this special honor that was being shown to Simon.

"Gee, I wish mother and father could be here." There was a wistful note in the boy's voice.

"Maybe they will," Uncle Phil began, but was stopped by a warning look in Aunt Elsa's eyes.

"You mustn't count on it, Simon dear," his aunt said. "It's true, they're on their way home and may possibly be here on time. But don't expect it, for the chances are that you'll be disappointed if you do."

"The boat is scheduled to dock the day before Shovuos," Mrs. Jonathon said to her husband when the children had left the room. "But it may easily be delayed."

"I'll send them a cable anyhow, and tell them about Simon's Confirmation," Uncle Phil decided.

What fun and excitement it was, getting ready for Confirmation. Each of the boys received a new suit. Confirmation gifts began to come in. Preparations for the reception were begun. Simon and Maury were busy with special meetings of the Confirmation class, which was to conduct the services in the synagogue on the important day. Both boys had a part in the service.

When Shovuos eve came, the hurry and bustle ended. There was a feeling of peace and calmness in the air, as Aunt Elsa lit the holiday candles and recited the blessing. Dr. Jonathon came in from the synagogue services and chanted the Kiddush over the wine, with the family gathered around the table. They enjoyed the special meal which Aunt Elsa had prepared.

"These holiday evenings at home are very pleasant," Dr. Jonathon remarked contentedly, as the family settled themselves in the living room afterwards.

"You haven't told us a thing about Shovuos when you were a boy," cried Ruthie reproachfully.

"You haven't asked me," he reminded her. "Everyone has been too busy rushing around and getting ready for Confirmation. I feel as if the whole family is going to be confirmed tomorrow morning." The boys laughed. They knew that Dr. Jonathon was proud of the fact that they were in the Confirmation class.

"Well, this is the right time for telling stories," Ruthie reminded him. "It's Shovuos eve."

"Shovuos eve." He leaned back and closed his eyes. "I can picture it so clearly in my mind. Our little cottage home, with its delightful holy day atmosphere. The evening meal is over. It was a dairy meal, with cheese pancakes and other good things. It is a custom to eat dairy foods on Shovuos. The dishes have been cleared away and the candles on the table are burning low. The windows are open, and fragrant, mild breezes drift in from the woods. Father is reading the *Book of Ruth,* the beautiful story in the Bible which describes such lovely harvest

scenes. It is read in the synagogue on Shovuos because
Ruth, a daughter of the Moabites, accepted the Jewish religion. You know that Shovuos is the birthday of Judaism.
There is a tradition that David, a descendant of Ruth, was
born on Shovuos and also died on a Shovuos day.

"But father is not left long to read in peace. We clamor
for a story. For father's head is filled with the wonderful
stories found in the Talmud, and on holidays especially,
he can be coaxed into telling them. I can remember one
that he liked to tell on Shovuos."

"What is it?" Ruthie cried.

"Well, there is a story that before giving the Torah to
the Jews, God offered it to the other nations of the earth.
But they all refused it, because they didn't want the responsibility of living up to these laws and of teaching them
to others. They all found some excuse for not accepting
the offer, saying that it would interfere with their own way
of living too much.

"When the Torah was offered to the Jews, however,
they accepted it without even knowing its contents, so
great was their faith in God. Thus, Israel, of its own free
will, undertook this great task of bringing enlightenment
to the world.

"The story goes on to tell us how Mt. Sinai was chosen
for the historic scene. It seems that all the important mountain peaks were fighting for the honor of being the place

from which the Torah was to be given. Mt. Ararat, where
Noah's Ark is said to have landed, claimed the privilege
for this reason. Mt. Carmel and Mt. Hermon each thought
that they should have the honor. But Mt. Sinai said, 'These
other mountains are much higher and grander than I am.
Yet even the most lofty one is too low for such a great
event. How, then, could I expect to be the one!' But because Mt. Sinai was humble, it was chosen as the place for
the giving of the Torah."

"Simon, what are you so restless about?" Aunt Elsa interrupted. "You keep wriggling in that chair."

"I'm all excited about Confirmation tomorrow," the
boy admitted. "Uncle Phil, were you ever confirmed?"

"No," his uncle replied. "But I think it is a beautiful
ceremony. It was begun by Reform Jews. Now, many Conservative synagogues also have Confirmation services."

Aunt Elsa firmly sent the children to bed early. They
mustn't be sleepy and tired on Confirmation Day.

Shovuos was a beautiful, clear day. Simon and Maury,
accompanied by the rest of the family, were soon on their
way to the synagogue, feeling very much dressed up and
pleasantly important. If Simon gave a thought to his ab-
sent parents, no one knew it, except, perhaps, Aunt Elsa,
who could see a trace of sadness beneath his excitement.

The synagogue was beautiful with flowers and green
shrubbery, especially the altar. The boys and girls of the

Confirmation class were on the platform, looking their best. Soon the services began. The choir filled the spacious house of worship with the sacred melodies and hymns of Shovuos. The voices of the children, repeating the words of the service, sounded sweet and clear over the vast congregation. Here and there, a parent silently wiped away a tear as the boys and girls, led by the reverent voice of the rabbi, dedicated themselves to Jewish life.

"And now," Rabbi Golding said, "I have one more pleasant duty to perform. A special honor is bestowed each year upon some member of the Confirmation class who has made the most outstanding progress during the year. I am happy to bestow this prize, the Bible and Prayer Book, beautifully bound, on one of these children sitting here before you."

There was a breathless silence as the rabbi paused. Simon looked out over the vast congregation. Then his heart gave a great leap. For there, standing in back of the last row of seats, were his father and mother. They must have just entered. Too bad they hadn't heard him say his part in the service, Simon thought, but was very excited and happy that they were here.

Suddenly he heard the rabbi pronounce his name. "This honor has been give to Simon Levy. Come forward, Simon."

The bewildered boy almost had to be pulled out of his

seat by his friendly neighbors. As he received the prize, Simon looked towards his parents and smiled. Would he ever forget this thrilling moment!

"Well," he said later, as he flew from his mother's embrace to his father's, "Shovuos is one holiday which I'll never forget."

THINGS TO DO AND TALK ABOUT
SHOVUOS

Reviewing the Story

1. Of what important historic event does Shovuos remind us?
2. Describe the diorama in the story, that deals with this event.
3. In ancient times, how was the Jewish belief in God different from the religious beliefs of other nations?
4. What other meaning does Shovuos have for us?
5. Describe one of the dioramas in the story that brings out this meaning.
6. What interesting ceremony is observed in modern Palestine as a part of the Shovuos celebration? On what biblical ceremony is it based?
7. Why is Shovuos a fitting name for the Confirmation ceremony? By what group in Jewish life was this ceremony started?
8. According to the legend, why did the other nations refuse the Torah? Why was Mt. Sinai chosen for the giving of the Torah, according to this same legend?

For Classroom Conversation

1. The belief in one God and the Ten Commandments are important contributions made by the Jews to world civilization. What improvements would there be in the world today if people really lived up to the ancient Jewish ideals?
2. What other Jewish festival that you have studied has both a historic meaning and an agricultural basis?
3. Our ancestors at Mt. Sinai accepted a great responsibility. What has this to do with our lives as Jews today?

4. Are there any advantages in having responsibilities and carrying them out? Discuss. Give examples of times when you had a special responsibility and tell how it affected you.

Suggested Activities

1.

Making Dioramas—Make the dioramas described in the story. If you haven't time to make them all, perhaps the whole class could work on a very large diorama showing Moses coming down Mt. Sinai with the Ten Commandments, and the children of Israel standing at the foot of the mountain.

2.

A Shovuos Processional—Plan a pageant for the whole school in which offerings will be made for the poor of the community or some other good cause. The altar in the synagogue should be decorated with flowers, green plants, and fruits. Each child in the procession should carry some offering of fruit or flowers. As the procession moves towards the altar, chant Psalm One Hundred. As each child brings up his offering, he may recite a verse from the *Psalms* which fits the occasion. Many such verses will be found in Psalms 65–92, 104–147, and others. A child dressed as the High Priest should receive the offerings and lay them around the altar. The children may then take their places to the right and left of the altar. At the conclusion, chant Isaiah 2: 2–5.

If possible the children might be dressed in the simple, flowing garments of biblical times. Some of them might carry paper models of ancient musical instruments.

OTHER FASTS AND FEASTS

"I JUST can't think," complained Simon, passing a hand over his ruffled hair. "There isn't even the glimmer of an idea in my mind."

"But we've got to have something for tomorrow night. We shouldn't have waited so long." Maury's tone was equally despairing. He sat on his cot, knees drawn up, and stared gloomily at the other five boys of Bunk Three, known as the Gideonites. They occupied one of the twelve small cottages which made up the Synagogue Camp. The other boys, Stanley, Bob, and Marvin, were also on their cots, for it was the rest hour. Through the open, screened windows came the fragrant cool air of the Maine woods.

"Minor fasts and feasts!" Marvin, snub-nosed and freckled, spoke in a scornful tone. "What could be exciting about a subject like that? The other bunks got all the breaks. They had the important holidays."

"Yes, it's tough," Bob agreed, a perplexed look in his dark eyes. "But we just can't fall down on this job, fellows. We'd be disgraced forever."

"Sh-sh," warned Stanley. "Here comes our counsellor."

The boys stretched out on their beds and an unnatural silence prevailed as Uncle Jack, a young man of twenty-two, entered the cottage and smiled at the death-like stillness.

"All right, boys, the rest hour is over."

With one motion, the boys leaped from their cots. "Uncle Jack, you've got to help us," Simon implored. "We have only until tomorrow night to put on a show for the whole camp."

"I'm ready whenever you are," Uncle Jack assured the group.

"Let's go into a huddle then," Maury decided. "Here, Simon, take this paper and pencil. You're secretary."

The boys gathered in a little group on the steps in front of their bunk. "First," Maury suggested, "let's make a list of all the minor holidays that we are going to include."

"Just a minute, boys." Simon jumped up suddenly, scattering papers and pencil. "I have a wonderful idea—an inspiration." The others perked up their heads eagerly. Simon's ideas were not to be despised.

"This is how we can present our show," Simon spoke excitedly. "The Jewish Year could be represented as a mother. All the holidays are her children. Most of them are big and important. A Jewish child is speaking to the Jewish Year. She asks about the other children who are not so important but also belong to the calendar. Then the minor holidays are summoned by the Jewish Year and they tell about themselves."

"That's a great idea," Bob cried, turning a few cartwheels on the grass to express his approval.

"A very good plan, Simon," Uncle Jack agreed. "But we'll have to work fast. Let's list the holidays now. We might start with Rosh Hodesh, which occurs on the first day of each month. Next, we might have Tishoh B'Ov and other fast days. After that, we would take Hamisho Osor B'Shevot, and then end the program with Lag B'-Omer."

"Gosh, those names sound like Greek to me," Marvin exclaimed.

"They happen to be Hebrew, not Greek," Uncle Jack replied. "Now, how about it? Do you want me to explain the meaning of these holidays to you?"

"Of course we do," Simon cried, and the others chimed in their approval. "We're lucky we've got a counsellor who's studying to be a rabbi and knows all about these things," Simon added.

"All right, here goes." Uncle Jack stretched out his legs to a more comfortable position and clasped his hands behind his head. "Rosh Hodesh means *Head of the Month,* or the first day of the month. The appearance of the new moon marks the beginning of the Jewish calendar month.

In olden times, Rosh Hodesh used to be a rather important festival. No work was done on that day, and special ceremonies were performed in the Temple at Jerusalem."

"How is Rosh Hodesh observed today?" Maury asked.

"In the synagogues, a special prayer is recited on the Sabbath before Rosh Hodesh," Uncle Jack told him. "In this prayer, God is asked to bless the coming month with life, and peace, and gladness, and joy.

"Another ceremony of Rosh Hodesh is the blessing of the moon. A group of people usually take part in this together, sometimes a whole congregation. The ceremony takes place out of doors. A prayer of thanks to God is recited, and the new moon is greeted with joy. Then the people wish each other and all the people of Israel happiness in the month to come.

"On the day of Rosh Hodesh," Uncle Jack continued, special prayers from the *Book of Psalms* are recited in the synagogue. A portion of the Bible is read, just as on the Sabbath.

"In the countries of Eastern Europe, children always look forward to Rosh Hodesh—it's a half holiday from school for them."

"That's a great idea," Marvin declared. "I wish we had that custom here."

"In those same lands," Uncle Jack went on, "the women also keep Rosh Hodesh as a half holiday. They don't do any extra household tasks like sewing or washing clothes. This custom is followed in some Orthodox Jewish homes here, too."

"Maybe we should go on to the other holidays now," Simon suggested. "Which one are you going to tell us about next?"

"Tishoh B'Ov," Uncle Jack replied. "The name means the ninth day of the Jewish month of Ov, which usually occurs during August. This is a very sad day for the Jewish people. A number of the most tragic events in our history have occurred on this day. It is a time of mourning for the fall of Jerusalem and the destruction of the Temple, which took place in 586 B. C. At this time, the armies of Babylonia conquered the small land of Judea. The capital city fell to the invaders, the sacred Temple was destroyed, and the best families were led as captives to Babylonia.

"Later on, the Jews returned to Palestine and rebuilt the Temple. Then, more than six hundred years after the destruction of the First Temple, Palestine again was conquered. This time it was the Romans who, after a hard war, broke through the walls of Jerusalem and burned the Second Temple to the ground. That was in the year 70. Tishoh B'Ov is the anniversary of this event too.

"But that isn't all," Uncle Jack continued. "Tishoh B'Ov kept right on being a day of misfortune for the Jewish people. Sixty-two years later, the Jews were at war again with the Romans, making a final effort to regain their freedom. Their leader in the rebellion was the heroic Bar Cochba. At first, he was successful and regained much territory from the Romans. But finally the mighty Roman armies prevailed. Once more it was on Tishoh B'Ov that the final misfortune befell the Jews. Their last fortress, Bethar, fell to the Romans."

"What a day," sighed Marvin.

"And don't forget," Uncle Jack reminded them, "another sad event of Jewish history happened on this unfortunate day."

"I remember," Maury put in. "In the year 1492, the Jews were expelled from Spain on Tishoh B'Ov."

"Yes," nodded Uncle Jack.

"I guess I should tell you about the Three Weeks and the Nine Days together with Tishoh B'Ov." Uncle Jack seemed to be thinking aloud.

"Three Weeks and Nine Days!" Simon was very curious. "Of course we want to know about them, Uncle Jack."

"It is a period of mourning connected with events that happened during the siege of Jerusalem in the time of the Romans," Uncle Jack explained. "The Three Weeks' period starts with a day of fasting on the seventeenth day of the Jewish month, Tammuz, and lasts through Tishoh B'Ov. The last Nine Days of this period are especially sad ones.

"You see, during this period, the Romans were besieging Jerusalem, and practically the entire land of Judea was in the hands of the enemy. The Jews were enduring great suffering and many of their soldiers were killed. On the seventeenth of Tammuz, which is the first day of the Three Weeks, the daily sacrifices in the Temple had to be stopped. The siege had pressed so heavily around the Temple that supplies could not be obtained. That day was the last time that Jews have offered sacrifices in the Temple, or anywhere else."

"What about the Nine Days?" Simon reminded him.

"During these last nine days of the three-week period, the sufferings of the Jews reached the highest point," Uncle Jack told him. "That is why the Nine Days are observed more strictly as a time of mourning, and the last day, Tishoh B'Ov, is kept as a fast day by pious Orthodox Jews."

"But how are the Three Weeks and Nine Days kept as a time of mourning?" Stanley asked.

"A good question," Uncle Jack declared. "During the Three Weeks, no special celebrations are allowed. It has become a custom not to have any weddings during this time. Some Orthodox Jews will not put on a new article of clothing which they have not worn before. Some will not take haircuts. They will not listen to music or go to the theater. During the Nine Days, the rules become stricter.

Many Orthodox Jews do not eat meat during these days.

"Here in the United States," Uncle Jack went on, "most Jews do not observe the Three Weeks or the Nine Days very strictly. But in the countries of Eastern Europe, where many of our parents and grandparents grew up, and where millions of Jews are living today, this period of mourning is kept with great seriousness.

"Let us look in on a congregation in Eastern Europe, on the eve of Tishoh B'Ov. Only a few candles are burning and they shed a flickering, mournful light. The worshipers have removed their shoes, as a special sign of mourning. Some of them sit on low stools, others upon the ground. The cantor is leading them in chanting from the *Book of Lamentations* in the Bible. Mournfully, almost sobbingly, their voices rise and fall as they chant:

> " 'How doth the city sit solitary,
>   That was full of people,
>   How is she become as a widow!
>   She that was great among the nations,
>   And princess among the provinces,
>   How is she become tributary!
>   She weepeth sore in the night,
>   And her tears are on her cheeks;
>   She hath none to comfort her
>   Among all her lovers;

All her friends have dealt treacherously with her,
They are become her enemies.
Judah is gone into exile because of affliction,
And because of great servitude;
She dwelleth among the nations,
She findeth no rest.'

"All day, on Tishoh B'Ov," Uncle Jack continued, "the people fast, pray, and mourn for the ancient glories of Israel, and for the Temple of Jerusalem that is no more.

"But the Jews do not remain gloomy. Hope never deserts them. The Sabbath following Tishoh B'Ov is known as the *Sabbath Nachamu,* the Sabbath of Comfort. In the synagogue, the fortieth chapter of Isaiah is recited:

" 'Comfort ye, comfort ye My people,
Saith your God.
Bid Jerusalem take heart,
And proclaim unto her
That her time of service is accomplished,
That her guilt is paid off;
That she hath received of the Lord's hand
Double for all her sins.' "

"You make it sound almost as interesting as dad does," Maury said admiringly. "And you know it all by heart, too."

"Thank you for those kind words," Uncle Jack smiled.

"In the past, this period of sadness was also a period of hope and prayer for the rebuilding of the ancient homeland, Palestine. And we, today, are seeing that hope fulfilled.

"There are several other fast days on the Jewish calendar. One is the Fast of Gedaliah. It is a reminder of the period when the First Temple was destroyed by Babylonia. A governor of Palestine was appointed for the conquered land. This man was Gedaliah, a descendant of the royal house of David. The Jewish people rejoiced at this appointment for they hoped that Gedaliah might help to preserve a part of Jewish national life. But the new governor was assassinated, and with his death went the last hopes for Jewish independence. The people were so disappointed that they made the day of his death a day of fasting. This anniversary has been remembered ever since. It is an easy day to remember because it occurs right after the second day of Rosh Hashonoh.

"Then there is a day of fasting known as the Fast of Esther."

"Oh, I know about that one," Maury interrupted. "Isn't that in memory of Queen Esther? She fasted three days before appearing before King Ahasuerus to plead for the lives of the Jewish people."

"That's right," Uncle Jack nodded. "The Fast of Esther

is in honor of the brave Jewish Queen who risked her life for her people. It comes on the day before Purim."

"Can't we go on now to the cheerful holidays?" Stanley suggested.

"Yes," Uncle Jack assured him. "We're going to talk about Lag B'Omer. That is a happy festival day."

"What does the name mean?" Simon asked.

"It simply gives the date of the holiday in Hebrew—the thirty-third day of the Counting of the Omer. I'll have to explain that strange date. In ancient times, the Jews celebrated the harvest season by bringing a measure, or *omer,* of grain as an offering to God. They brought the first omer on the second day of Passover. They continued to bring an omer each day until exactly seven weeks had passed. On the fiftieth day, the festival of Shovuos was celebrated. Each day as they brought the omer of grain to the Temple, they counted the number of days since they had started. This is known as the *Counting of the Omer.* Lag B'Omer, then, is the thirty-third day of the Counting of the Omer."

"Then it must come sixteen days before Shovuos," Simon calculated."

"That's right," Uncle Jack told him. "Now I'll tell you what the holiday means and how it is celebrated. There are two interesting stories connected with this festival. Practically all of the minor holidays that we have been talking about go back to the period when the Jews were at war with the Romans. I have told you about Bar Cochba, the brave general who led the Jewish soldiers against the mighty Roman army. They were making a last gallant effort to regain their freedom. The great Rabbi Akiba, who lived at this time, encouraged and inspired Bar Cochba in his work. Akiba was a famous teacher, and many students came from distant places to study Torah with him. The Romans had forbidden the study of the Jewish religion, but Rabbi Akiba defied this decree. There is a story that during the days of the Counting of the Omer, a terrible epidemic broke out among the students of Akiba and many thousands died of the dreadful disease. During this same period, many Jewish soldiers were killed on the battlefield. It was indeed a very difficult time for the small nation of Judea, at war with mighty Rome. Therefore these weeks of the Counting of the Omer are remembered by Jews as a time of mourning. No weddings or other important celebrations are held by Orthodox Jews during this period. But we are told that on Lag B'Omer, the epidemic among the students of Akiba suddenly stopped. So this day stands out as a happy day in a dark period of suffering. Sometimes it is called *Scholars' Day,* in remembrance of the students of Akiba."

"That's a good story," Marvin declared. "Did you say you had two stories about Lag B'Omer?"

"Yes," Uncle Jack continued, "I want to tell you about another famous rabbi whose name is connected with this same holiday—Simeon Bar Yohai. He, also, refused to obey the Roman decree to stop teaching the Jewish religion to the many students who gathered around him. The time came, however, when he had to flee for his life from the pursuing Roman officers. Together with his small son, he went to Galilee. He found a hiding place high up among the hills, near the small village of Meron. There the father and son hid for thirteen years. Their home was a cave. Their food was the fruit of the carob tree and water from a spring. It is said that during these years in hiding, Rabbi Simeon Bar Yohai wrote the famous book known as the *Zohar,* which Jews study to this day.

"The story also tells us that each year, on Lag B'Omer, his students would visit him. In order to prevent the Romans from suspecting where they were going, the young men dressed as hunters, carrying bows and arrows in their hands. It is said that Rabbi Bar Yohai died on Lag B'Omer and was buried at Meron. He requested his students to observe the anniversary of his death as a happy day, rather than as a day of mourning."

"He was brave and bold, as well as being a scholar," Simon declared. "Something like Rabbi Akiba, wasn't he?"

"Yes," Uncle Jack replied, "except that Akiba's life

ended differently. Akiba died as a martyr at the hands of the Romans because he insisted on continuing his teaching of the Torah."

"How is Lag B'Omer celebrated?" Maury wanted to know.

"In Palestine, the largest celebration is held at Meron. People from all over the country come to this tiny settlement high up in the hills of Galilee. They gather around the tombs of Rabbi Bar Yohai and his son Eliezer. They build a bonfire and dance and sing around it from midnight until dawn."

"It sounds very jolly," Stanley said.

"Lag B'Omer is celebrated all over Palestine," Uncle Jack continued. "It is a day for picnics and outdoor activities for the schoolchildren. Games and contests are often held on this day. In the evening, bonfires are lit, both in cities and in colonies. Young people gather around them to dance and sing joyously, and to listen to stories of Simeon Bar Yohai, Rabbi Akiba, and the heroic events of the days in which they lived."

"Why can't we celebrate Lag B'Omer like that?" demanded Simon. "I think it would be lots of fun."

"Many Jewish schools and clubs do celebrate this holiday here just as it is done in Palestine," Uncle Jack assured him. "Let's remember to do it next spring when Lag B'Omer comes around."

"I'll mark it off on my calendar," Simon declared. "It's on the thirty-third day from the second day of Passover. That's easy."

"You'll be counting the days of the Omer, then," Uncle Jack told him, "just as Jews have done since ancient times. But, of course, you can find Lag B'Omer marked on any Jewish calendar."

"If father were here, he could tell us how he used to celebrate Lag B'Omer in Lithuania, when he was a boy," Maury remarked.

"I can tell you one or two things about it," Uncle Jack replied. "Then, too, this festival was celebrated outdoors as a picnic day. The schoolchildren usually went with their teachers. They took their lunch along and spent the whole

day in the woods. Sometimes they would dress up as hunters and play games at archery and warfare. This was in
memory of the disguise worn by the students of Bar Yohai,
and also because of the days of warfare with the Romans,
which this holiday recalls."

"Are you going to tell us about other holidays?" Stanley
asked.

"Just one more," Uncle Jack answered, "and I think
you'll enjoy hearing about it. It is a happy holiday and is
beloved by children, just like Lag B'Omer. It is also celebrated chiefly outdoors. This holiday is Hamisho Osor
B'Shevat."

"I can't even pronounce that name," Marvin protested.
"What does it mean?"

"It means the Fifteenth Day of the Jewish month of
Shevat," Uncle Jack said. "This holiday comes in mid-

winter, usually February, and is also known as the *New Year of the Trees."*

"Isn't that the day on which you eat all kinds of fruit that grow in Palestine, especially *bokser,* or, what do you call it—St. John's bread?" Maury asked.

"That's right," Uncle Jack told him. "Hamisho Osor B'Shevat marks the coming of spring in Palestine. In this country we are still in the midst of winter when we celebrate this Jewish Arbor Day. But in the milder climate of Palestine, the rainy season is about over, spring flowers begin to come up, and the trees start to blossom.

"The Jewish people have always loved and appreciated trees," Uncle Jack continued. "The Bible is full of references to trees. The prophets talk about the time when each man shall sit under his own vine and fig tree. The psalms often mention trees. 'He shall be like a tree that is planted by streams of water.'

"The Talmud has some charming stories about trees. One of them tells of an old man, past seventy, who was planting a carob tree by the wayside. A young man stopped to watch him and said, 'Grandsire, why do you bother to plant that tree? Don't you know that it takes seventy years for a carob tree to bear fruit? You will never be able to enjoy the results of your labor.'

"The old man looked at him and replied, 'During my lifetime I have eaten the fruits of trees that others have planted. Shall I not do as much for those who come after me? It is happiness enough to be able to provide for our children and children's children.' Then the young man was ashamed and walked thoughtfully away.

"It is interesting," Uncle Jack went on, "that in all the centuries that Jews were away from Palestine, they continued to observe this New Year of the Trees. The Jews in the Middle Ages, living in crowded ghettos, still remembered to celebrate Hamisho Osor B'Shevat. They looked forward to the time when the Jews would once more return to Palestine and plant trees in the ancient homeland."

"I read an interesting story not long ago," Simon remarked. "It told how Hamisho Osor B'Shevat was celebrated in Palestine. But I don't remember it very well. Can you tell us about it, Uncle Jack?"

"Modern Palestine has put new life and meaning into this ancient festival," Uncle Jack told him. "Trees are having an important part in making Palestine once more into a fruitful and beautiful land. I don't need to tell you how important trees are in any land. In Palestine, they are particularly necessary. They help to keep the thin soil in place on the hillsides. They help to drain swamps which breed malaria. They provide shade in a subtropical climate. No wonder that Hamisho Osor B'Shevat is a beloved holiday in Palestine."

"How do they celebrate it there?" Maury asked. "You were in Palestine, so I guess you know."

"The children have a large share in the celebration," Uncle Jack said. "Of course, the planting of trees is an important part of the events of the day."

"Just like Arbor Day here in the United States," put in Marvin.

"Yes. Well, let us imagine that it is the day of the festival and we are in the city of Tel Aviv. Although it is February, the sun is pleasantly warm and the air is mild. There is a stir of excitement about the city. Let us follow that group of marching schoolchildren who sing joyously as they parade through the streets. After awhile, we find ourselves on the outskirts of the city, where a new suburb is being built. Trees are to be planted along the main street, which is still unpaved. Now the street is filled with marching children, each one wearing a green wreath on his head. They carry spades, hoes, and sprinkling cans. Each group has one or two banners which rise high into the air. On the banners are proverbs and pictures about trees.

"And now the crowd gathers around a decorated platform which has been erected for this occasion. The sound of the bugle calls everyone to attention. Several youths ascend the platform. They are dressed in the flowing white costume of the priests of ancient Israel. They unfold a scroll and read together the proclamation for Hamisho Osor B'Shevat bidding the people to plant all kinds of trees.

"From the crowd of children comes the sturdy response, 'We are here, ready to plant.'

" 'Strength and courage to you,' those on the platform reply. And now children and adults join in singing songs. The children then march past the platform to receive the saplings which they are to plant. The band is playing, the children singing, and they march around and around the platform, carrying their young trees and tools for planting.

"The exact spots where the trees are to be planted have been marked. A group gathers around each of these places. Some dig, others hurry off to get the water. Soon the sapling is set carefully into the ground and its roots are firmly covered with earth. Water streams upon it from the sprinkling cans. The work is soon accomplished.

"At a signal, the band strikes up the tune of a planting song. Each group joins hands around the newly-planted tree. They dance and sing gaily."

"It must be lots of fun," Simon cried. "I'd like to be there and take part in that ceremony."

"But how do the children here celebrate this holiday?" Stanley asked.

"Many of the Jewish schools have parties and entertainments," Uncle Jack replied. "The story of Palestine and its trees have a large part on the program. Fruits are served

for refreshments, especially those that grow in Palestine, such as dates, figs, raisins, and oranges. As Simon told you, the most popular fruit for this holiday is St. John's bread."

"Well, we certainly have enough material now for our show," Simon declared. "Gee, Uncle Jack, you've been swell."

"Now we have to figure out just how we will present each minor holiday when the Jewish Year calls him," Maury reminded them.

As the boys reviewed the meaning of each holiday, ideas

for their show came thick and fast, and their enthusiasm grew.

The next evening, when all the campers gathered in the assembly room, the Gideonites put on their play about minor feasts and fasts. In the care-free spirit of the Camp Theater, the players could change their lines or add to them as they went along. Their play turned out to be one of the best of the season and won them much applause.

THINGS TO DO AND TALK ABOUT
OTHER FASTS AND FEASTS

Reviewing the Story

On a sheet of paper, write the name of the minor festival which describes each of the following groups of words. Use the list given below. Number your answers to match the group of words described.

Tishoh B'Ov—Three Weeks—Nine Days—Rosh Hodesh— Lag B'Omer—Hamisho Osor B'Shevat—Fast of Gedaliah— Fast of Esther

1. When the *Book of Lamentations* is chanted in the synagogue.
2. Has the number *33* in its name.
3. Is called the *New Year of the Trees*.
4. Is celebrated by picnics and bonfire parties.
5. Comes every month.
6. A day on which great misfortunes have occurred to the Jewish people in widely-separated centuries.
7. The name means *Head of the Month*.
8. Is sometimes called *Scholars' Day*.
9. A period occurring during the latter part of the Three Weeks.
10. The last day of the Three Weeks.
11. Is associated with the name of Simeon Bar Yohai.
12. A fast day which comes just before Purim.
13. Is celebrated in Palestine by the planting of trees.
14. A day on which it is customary to eat Palestine fruit.

15. A fast day which occurs right after Rosh Hashonoh.
16. A period of half-mourning starting with the seventeenth day of Tammuz.
17. Comes in midwinter in this country.
18. A fast day which occurs during the summer season.
19. Is celebrated by a ceremony called the *Blessing of the Moon*.
20. Occurs on the ninth day of the month.

For Classroom Conversation

1. Which of these minor festivals do you observe, either at home, school, or in some club? How do you observe them?
2. Which of these holidays would you particularly like to observe? How?

Suggested Activities

1.

Draw large pictures illustrating these holidays.

2.

Make up a play about the minor festivals, like the play described in the story.

3.

Plan to observe Lag B'Omer and Hamisho Osor B'Shevat in religious school, when these holidays occur.

THE JEWISH HOLIDAYS ON PARADE

WHAT are you doing over here?" Maury regarded his sister Ruthie with displeasure as he gave a last tug to the bed he was making. "Don't you know you're out of bounds, coming over to the boys' camp this way?"

Ruthie sat down on Simon's bed and swung her legs. "This is the last day of camp so the boundary rules won't be enforced," she told him calmly. "Where is Simon? I want him to help me with my costume for this afternoon."

"Somewhere around. I don't know. This camp is certainly like a three-ring circus today. Parents all over the place." Maury's tone was plainly disapproving.

"I like it this way—it's fun," Ruthie declared. "But I mustn't sit here wasting time. I'm going to be one of the handmaidens of Sukkos in the pageant."

"I won't tell you about my part," Maury decided. "I want to surprise mother and daddy, so it'll be safer not to tell you."

"Well—" Ruthie began indignantly, but stopped as

215

Simon burst through the doorway, flushed and excited. In his hand he waved a pencil and notebook.

"Hi," he called out, dropping on the bed next to Ruthie.

"What are those for?" the little girl demanded. "What part are you going to have in the *Jewish Holidays on Parade?* Will you help me with my costume? Where are mother and daddy and your parents? Why don't you answer my questions?"

"Whoa, there," laughed Simon. "With which one should I begin? The parents, all four of them, are going on a special tour of the camp grounds. The director told me confidentially that was the only method to keep them out of the way and out of mischief. Now what's next, let me see. I'm not going to have any part in the parade."

"Oh, Simon, I thought everyone was in it." Ruthie's tone was distressed. "Are you being punished?"

"No," her cousin assured her. "I have something lots more interesting to do. I am the special correspondent of the *Synagogue Camp Paper.*" He waved his notebook and pencil. "My job is to watch the entire pageant and write it up for the camp magazine."

"How exciting," Maury cried. "Will it really be printed, Simon?"

"Yes, if it's good enough. Come on, Ruthie, I think I have an idea for your costume."

After hours of excited preparation, the children of the

camp were ready for the big event. The parade, headed by the camp band, was to proceed across the athletic field, down the pathway in front of the cottages, and along the grassy level by the edge of the lake.

"Come, mother, let's sit here," Simon suggested, leading the way to a rustic bench by the side of the road. "We'll get a good view here. Sit down, Aunt Elsa. You, too, dad and Uncle Phil. I'll sit on the grass here."

"You're a fine host, my boy." His father smiled at him.

"I guess you'll have to explain things to me, Simon." His mother's tone was a bit apologetic. "I'm afraid I don't know much about the Jewish holidays. But now that you've gotten so interested in them, I'd like to learn too."

"All right, mother, I'll stick by you," he promised gravely.

After what seemed like endless waiting to the crowds of parents and guests, there came the welcome sound of the band playing the camp song. The parade had begun, headed by the lively leader of the band.

Simon's mother, Mrs. Levy, stood up and craned her neck to see the beginning. "Who is the beautiful girl dressed in flowing white and wearing the crown?" she asked. "See, she is marching directly after the band."

"That is Rosh Hashonoh, the head of the year," Simon told her. "Listen, she is blowing the shofar. Notice how serious she is. Rosh Hashonoh is a solemn festival on which

Jews pray for a good year to come. They resolve to lead better lives than they did in the past."

"Rather different from the way we usher in January first," his mother said thoughtfully.

"The ten maidens in white who are following, two by two," Simon went on, after scribbling some notes in his book, "are the Ten Days of Penitence, from Rosh Hashonoh to Yom Kippur. They are the days of grace during which the Jews may repent of their wrongdoings of the past year and be forgiven."

"I suppose the girl right in back of them is Yom Kippur," Mrs. Levy remarked. "What a lovely, flowing white gown she has on! But why is she carrying that large quill pen and an open book?"

"That is the Book of Judgment," Uncle Phil told her. "According to an old belief, each one's fate for the coming year is decided on Yom Kippur."

"Look," cried Aunt Elsa, "there is Ruthie, right behind the tall girl—the one who is wearing a garland of flowers and carrying a cornucopia of fruit. She must be Sukkos and Ruthie is one of her handmaidens. Doesn't the child look sweet with those brightly-colored leaves pinned all over her white dress?"

"You'd think she looked sweet even if she were wearing torn overalls," laughed Dr. Jonathon, putting an arm affectionately around his wife.

"And so she would," Aunt Elsa declared. "My goodness, Simon, how fast you're scribbling in that notebook. 'Handmaidens dancing gaily along behind Sukkos,' she read over his shoulder. 'The harvest festival of thanksgiving.'"

"Oh, look, mother," Simon cried. "That's a miniature sukkah which the boys are carrying on a platform, right in back of the handmaidens. The boys made it themselves."

"Why, there's Naomi sitting in front of it, riding along like a little princess," exclaimed Dr. Jonathon, delighted.

"Hello, darling," her mother waved.

"That band plays very well," Mr. Levy remarked. "It makes the procession quite lively."

"Simon," his mother asked, "why is that boy carrying a scroll of the Torah? See, he is marching right behind the Sukkos procession."

"He is Simhas Torah, the day of Rejoicing in the Law," the boy explained. "You know that a portion of the Torah is read in the synagogue each week, on the Sabbath. On Simhas Torah, which follows right after Sukkos, the reading of the entire Torah is completed and then begun again."

"The next part of the parade is about Hanukah," Aunt Elsa announced. "There go Mattathias and his sons. Why look, Phil, our boy is Judah Maccabee. How nice! So that's the surprise he was talking about. Doesn't he look grand!"

"That large Menorah the boys are carrying is beautiful," Mr. Levy remarked.

Behind the Menorah, eight little girls wearing yellow, pointed caps danced gaily along. They were, of course, the eight Hanukah candles.

"Who are all those interesting-looking characters who come next?" Mrs. Levy wanted to know. "Oh, don't tell me—I think I remember. They are connected with Purim. See, there is Queen Esther walking with the king—what's his name?"

"Ahasuerus," Dr. Jonathon reminded her. "That fine-looking old man in front of them is Mordecai, her uncle. It was his influence that inspired Esther to plead with the king that the lives of the Jews should be saved. For that wicked Haman, who is walking last, plotted to destroy them."

"I think the next part of the parade is one of the most interesting," Simon put in as he stopped writing for a moment. "It's about Passover. There is Moses leading his people out of Egypt. See, the mothers are holding the little children by the hand and the fathers are walking along with heavy sacks of household goods swung over their shoulders."

"Very well done," Dr. Jonathon agreed.

"There is a family at a Seder," Aunt Elsa cried. "How

clever to put it on a platform and carry it that way. Those cardboard figures look very life-like."

"What is the next part about, Uncle Phil?" Simon begged. "I'm writing so fast, I haven't time to look."

"A very fine Moses carrying the Ten Commandments," Uncle Phil told him. "About Shovuos, you know. The Children of Israel are following him. Right after, there is a procession of Jews bearing the first fruits of the land to the Temple, as they used to do in Palestine in ancient times. Shovuos is also a harvest festival, you remember."

"Thanks, uncle, that was fine."

"Who is that tragic figure coming next?" asked Mrs. Levy as she watched a young girl dressed in sackcloth and weeping sadly.

"She is Tishoh B'Ov," Simon explained. "That is the day on which the Temple in Jerusalem was destroyed on two different occasions, centuries apart. Other terrible things happened to the Jewish people on that day, during different periods of their history."

"The next part is clever," chuckled Uncle Phil. A number of smaller children were walking along, carrying a sign.

"Protect the minors," read Mrs. Levy. "I can't quite see how that fits in."

"Read the names they have printed on the bands across their chests," Mr. Levy advised.

"You read them," his wife retorted.

"The first is Rosh Hodesh," Dr. Jonathon put in. "That means the first day of the new month. The next one is Hamisho Osor B'Shevat, which is the holiday known as the New Year of the Trees. The next one is Lag B'Omer, in memory of certain famous men who lived in the time of the Bar Cochba revolt."

"But I still don't understand that sign," Mrs. Levy insisted.

"Most people are inclined to forget these minor festivals," Uncle Phil told her, "so we must help to 'protect the minors.'"

"Look, mother," Simon interrupted, "the last part is about the Sabbath. That girl with the long dress and crown is the Queen Sabbath. Behind her comes a Jew. He is escorted on each side by an angel of peace."

"Beautiful," his mother agreed.

"I must congratulate your director," Dr. Jonathon said. "I have really enjoyed the *Jewish Holidays on Parade*."

THINGS TO DO AND TALK ABOUT
THE JEWISH HOLIDAYS ON PARADE

Reviewing the Story

Write the name of a holiday from the following list which best describes each group of words given below. If the words describe more than one holiday, choose the one most closely connected with the description given.

Rosh Hashonoh—Yom Kippur—Sukkos—Simhas Torah—Hanukah—Hamisho Osor B'Shevat—Purim—Lag B'Omer—Passover—Shovuos—Tishoh B'Ov—Sabbath—Rosh Hodesh

1. Blowing the shofar
2. Eating matzo
3. The tablets of the Law
4. Fasting
5. The New Year
6. Day of mourning
7. Re-dedication of the Temple
8. Blessing the moon
9. Day of rest
10. Afikomon
11. Eating in a booth
12. Tashlich
13. The New Year of the Trees
14. Asking forgiveness for wrongs done
15. Scholars' day
16. Offering of the First Fruits
17. Seder

18. Confirmation Day
19. Lighting eight candles
20. The Exodus from Egypt
21. Blessing the candles
22. Harvest festival
23. Havdoloh
24. Reading the Megillah
25. Rejoicing in the Law
26. Esrog and lulov

Suggested Activities

1.

Present a pageant of *The Jewish Holidays on Parade,* as described in the story.[1]

2.

Make a frieze showing a moving pageant of figures which describe the holidays. Follow the description in the story, if you like.

---

[1] Note to Teacher: See the play, *The Jewish Holidays on Parade,* by Dorothy F. Zeligs, for supplementary material in connection with this chapter.

BLESSINGS USED THROUGHOUT THE STORY

In English and Hebrew

ROSH HASHONOH

Lighting the Candles

Blessed art Thou, O Lord our God, King of the Universe, who hast sanctified us by thy commandments and commanded us to kindle the holy day lights.

Blessed art Thou, O Lord our God, who hast given us life and hast preserved us, and enabled us to reach this season.

(*This blessing is used when lighting the candles at the beginning of each holiday.*)

בָּרוּךְ אַתָּה יְיָ אֱלֹהֵינוּ מֶלֶךְ הָעוֹלָם. אֲשֶׁר קִדְּשָׁנוּ בְּמִצְוֹתָיו וְצִוָּנוּ לְהַדְלִיק נֵר שֶׁל יוֹם טוֹב:

בָּרוּךְ אַתָּה יְיָ אֱלֹהֵינוּ מֶלֶךְ הָעוֹלָם. שֶׁהֶחֱיָנוּ וְקִיְּמָנוּ וְהִגִּיעָנוּ לַזְּמַן הַזֶּה:

Kiddush

See The Sabbath, page 230.

When Eating Bread

Blessed art Thou, O Lord our God, King of the Universe, who bringest forth bread from the earth.

226

בָּרוּךְ אַתָּה יְיָ אֱלֹהֵינוּ מֶלֶךְ הָעוֹלָם. הַמּוֹצִיא לֶחֶם מִן הָאָרֶץ:

When Eating Fruit

Blessed art Thou, O Lord our God, King of the Universe, who bringest forth fruit from the earth.

בָּרוּךְ אַתָּה יְיָ אֱלֹהֵינוּ מֶלֶךְ הָעוֹלָם. בּוֹרֵא פְּרִי הָעֵץ:

When Eating Honey on Rosh Hashonoh

May it be thy will, O Lord our God and God of our fathers, to renew unto us a sweet and pleasant year.

יְהִי רָצוֹן מִלְפָנֶיךָ יְיָ אֱלֹהֵינוּ וֵאלֹהֵי אֲבוֹתֵינוּ שֶׁתְּחַדֵּשׁ עָלֵינוּ שָׁנָה טוֹבָה וּמְתוּקָה:

Greetings for the New Year

May you be inscribed for a happy New Year.

לְשָׁנָה טוֹבָה תִּכָּתֵבוּ.

YOM KIPPUR

Lighting the Candles

בָּרוּךְ אַתָּה יְיָ אֱלֹהֵינוּ מֶלֶךְ הָעוֹלָם. אֲשֶׁר קִדְּשָׁנוּ בְּמִצְוֹתָיו וְצִוָּנוּ לְהַדְלִיק נֵר שֶׁל יוֹם הַכִּפּוּרִים:

(See Rosh Hashonoh, page 226, for second part.)

Kiddush

See The Sabbath, page 230.

Blessing the Children

See The Sabbath, page 229–230.

SUKKOS

A Blessing Recited in the Sukkah

Blessed art Thou, O Lord our God, King of the Universe, who hast sanctified us by thy commandments and commanded us to sit in the sukkah.

Blessed art Thou, O Lord our God, who hast given us life and hast preserved us, and enabled us to reach this season.

בָּרוּךְ אַתָּה יְיָ אֱלֹהֵינוּ מֶלֶךְ הָעוֹלָם. אֲשֶׁר קִדְּשָׁנוּ בְּמִצְוֹתָיו
וְצִוָּנוּ לֵישֵׁב בַּסֻּכָּה:

בָּרוּךְ אַתָּה יְיָ אֱלֹהֵינוּ מֶלֶךְ הָעוֹלָם. שֶׁהֶחֱיָנוּ וְקִיְּמָנוּ
וְהִגִּיעָנוּ לַזְּמַן הַזֶּה:

Blessing Said Over the Four Species

Blessed art Thou, O Lord our God, King of the Universe, who hast commanded us to take the lulov.

Blessed art Thou, O God, King of the Universe, who

hast given us life and hast preserved us, and enabled us to reach this season.

בָּרוּךְ אַתָּה יְיָ אֱלֹהֵינוּ מֶלֶךְ הָעוֹלָם. אֲשֶׁר קִדְּשָׁנוּ בְּמִצְוֹתָיו
וְצִוָּנוּ עַל־נְטִילַת לוּלָב:

בָּרוּךְ אַתָּה יְיָ אֱלֹהֵינוּ מֶלֶךְ הָעוֹלָם. שֶׁהֶחֱיָנוּ וְקִיְּמָנוּ
וְהִגִּיעָנוּ לַזְּמָן הַזֶּה:

THE SABBATH

Lighting the Candles

Blessed art Thou, O Lord our God, King of the Universe, who hast sanctified us by thy commandments and commanded us to kindle the Sabbath lights.

בָּרוּךְ אַתָּה יְיָ אֱלֹהֵינוּ מֶלֶךְ הָעוֹלָם. אֲשֶׁר קִדְּשָׁנוּ בְּמִצְוֹתָיו
וְצִוָּנוּ לְהַדְלִיק נֵר שֶׁל־שַׁבָּת:

Welcoming the Sabbath

Come, my friend, to meet the bride,
Let us welcome the Sabbath day.

לְכָה דוֹדִי לִקְרַאת כַּלָּה. פְּנֵי שַׁבָּת נְקַבְּלָה.

Blessing the Children

(*For Boys*) God make thee like Ephraim and Manasseh.
(*For Girls*) God make thee like Sarah, Rebecca, Rachel, and Leah.

The Lord bless thee and keep thee. The Lord make His face to shine upon thee and be gracious unto thee. The Lord turn His face unto thee and give thee peace. Amen.

(For Boys)   יְשִׂמְךָ אֱלֹהִים כְּאֶפְרַיִם וְכִמְנַשֶּׁה:

(For Girls)   יְשִׂמֵךְ אֱלֹהִים כְּשָׂרָה רִבְקָה רָחֵל וְלֵאָה:

יְבָרֶכְךָ יְיָ וְיִשְׁמְרֶךָ. יָאֵר יְיָ פָּנָיו אֵלֶיךָ וִיחֻנֶּךָּ. יִשָּׂא יְיָ פָּנָיו אֵלֶיךָ וְיָשֵׂם לְךָ שָׁלוֹם:

Kiddush

And it was evening and it was morning, the sixth day.

And the heavens and the earth were finished and all their hosts. And on the seventh day, God had finished His work which He had made, and He rested on the seventh day from all His work which He had made. And God blessed the seventh day and hallowed it, because He rested thereon from all His work which God had created and made.

Blessed art Thou, O Lord our God, King of the Universe, creator of the fruit of the vine.

Blessed art Thou, O Lord our God, King of the Universe, who hast sanctified us by thy commandments and hast taken pleasure in us, and in love and favor hast given us thy holy Sabbath as an inheritance.

Blessed art Thou, O Lord, who hallowest the Sabbath.

*(The Kiddush given above has been somewhat short-
ened. For changes made in the Kiddush on various holidays, see The Standard Prayer Book, Bloch Publishing
Co.)*

וַיְהִי־עֶרֶב וַיְהִי בֹקֶר

יוֹם הַשִּׁשִּׁי וַיְכֻלוּ הַשָּׁמַיִם וְהָאָרֶץ וְכָל צְבָאָם: וַיְכַל אֱלֹהִים
בַּיוֹם הַשְּׁבִיעִי מְלַאכְתּוֹ אֲשֶׁר עָשָׂה וַיִּשְׁבֹּת בַּיוֹם הַשְּׁבִיעִי
מִכָּל־מְלַאכְתּוֹ אֲשֶׁר עָשָׂה: וַיְבָרֶךְ אֱלֹהִים אֶת־יוֹם הַשְּׁבִיעִי
וַיְקַדֵּשׁ אֹתוֹ. כִּי בוֹ שָׁבַת מִכָּל־מְלַאכְתּוֹ אֲשֶׁר־בָּרָא אֱלֹהִים
לַעֲשׂוֹת:

בָּרוּךְ אַתָּה יְיָ אֱלֹהֵינוּ מֶלֶךְ הָעוֹלָם. בּוֹרֵא פְּרִי הַגָּפֶן:

בָּרוּךְ אַתָּה יְיָ אֱלֹהֵינוּ מֶלֶךְ הָעוֹלָם. אֲשֶׁר קִדְּשָׁנוּ בְּמִצְוֹתָיו
וְרָצָה בָנוּ. וְשַׁבַּת קָדְשׁוֹ בְּאַהֲבָה וּבְרָצוֹן הִנְחִילָנוּ זִכָּרוֹן
לְמַעֲשֵׂה בְרֵאשִׁית. כִּי הוּא יוֹם תְּחִלָּה לְמִקְרָאֵי קֹדֶשׁ זֵכֶר
לִיצִיאַת מִצְרָיִם. כִּי בָנוּ בָחַרְתָּ וְאוֹתָנוּ קִדַּשְׁתָּ מִכָּל־הָעַמִּים
וְשַׁבַּת קָדְשְׁךָ בְּאַהֲבָה וּבְרָצוֹן הִנְחַלְתָּנוּ. בָּרוּךְ אַתָּה יְיָ.
מְקַדֵּשׁ הַשַּׁבָּת:

Havdoloh

Behold, God is my salvation. I will trust and not be
afraid, for the Lord is my strength and my song. He is
also become my salvation and ye shall draw water with
joy from the fountains of salvation. Salvation is with the
Lord. May thy blessing be upon thy people. The Lord of

Hosts is with us. The Lord of Jacob is our refuge. The Jews were once favored with delight and joy, gladness and honor. Thus may it also be with us.

I will lift up the cup of salvation and call upon the name of the Lord. Blessed art Thou, O Lord our God, King of the Universe, creator of the fruit of the vine.

(Puts down goblet and recites:)

Blessed art Thou, O Lord our God, who createst various kinds of spices. (Inhales the fragrance of the spices. Holds hands towards the light and turns fingers over palms, causing a shadow to fall.)

Blessed art Thou, O Lord our God, who createst the light of the fire.

Blessed art Thou, O Lord our God, King of the Universe, who hast made a distinction between things sacred and profane, between light and darkness, between Israel and other nations, between the seventh day and the six days of labor. Blessed art Thou, O Lord, who hast made a distinction between things sacred and profane.

(*For holidays, omit the blessing of God as creator of light. On night of Yom Kippur, omit the blessing over the spices, unless the holiday occurs on a Saturday.*)

הִנֵּה אֵל יְשׁוּעָתִי אֶבְטַח וְלֹא אֶפְחָד כִּי עָזִּי וְזִמְרָת יָהּ יְיָ
וַיְהִי־לִי לִישׁוּעָה: וּשְׁאַבְתֶּם מַיִם בְּשָׂשׂוֹן מִמַּעַיְנֵי הַיְשׁוּעָה: לַיְיָ
הַיְשׁוּעָה עַל־עַמְּךָ בִרְכָתֶךָ סֶּלָה: יְיָ צְבָאוֹת עִמָּנוּ מִשְׂנָּב־לָנוּ

אֱלֹהֵי יַעֲקֹב סֶלָה: לַיְּהוּדִים הָיְתָה אוֹרָה וְשִׂמְחָה וְשָׂשׂוֹן וִיקָר:

כֵּן תִּהְיֶה לָּנוּ: כּוֹס יְשׁוּעוֹת אֶשָּׂא וּבְשֵׁם יְיָ אֶקְרָא:

בָּרוּךְ אַתָּה יְיָ אֱלֹהֵינוּ מֶלֶךְ הָעוֹלָם. בּוֹרֵא פְּרִי הַגָּפֶן:

בָּרוּךְ אַתָּה יְיָ אֱלֹהֵינוּ מֶלֶךְ הָעוֹלָם. בּוֹרֵא מִינֵי בְשָׂמִים:

בָּרוּךְ אַתָּה יְיָ אֱלֹהֵינוּ מֶלֶךְ הָעוֹלָם. בּוֹרֵא מְאוֹרֵי הָאֵשׁ:

בָּרוּךְ אַתָּה יְיָ אֱלֹהֵינוּ מֶלֶךְ הָעוֹלָם. הַמַּבְדִּיל בֵּין קֹדֶשׁ

לְחוֹל בֵּין אוֹר לְחֹשֶׁךְ בֵּין יִשְׂרָאֵל לָעַמִּים. בֵּין יוֹם הַשְּׁבִיעִי

לְשֵׁשֶׁת יְמֵי הַמַּעֲשֶׂה. בָּרוּךְ אַתָּה יְיָ. הַמַּבְדִּיל בֵּין קֹדֶשׁ לְחוֹל:

HANUKAH

Lighting the Hanukah Lights

Blessed art Thou, O Lord our God, King of the Universe, who hast sanctified us by thy commandments and commanded us to kindle the lights of Hanukah.

Blessed art Thou, O Lord our God, King of the Universe, who performed miracles for our fathers in days of old, at this season.

Blessed art Thou, O Lord our God, King of the Universe, who hast kept us in life and hast preserved us, and enabled us to reach this season.

(*The above prayer is somewhat shortened. For the full prayer, see The Standard Prayer Book, Bloch Publishing Co.*)

בָּרוּדְ אַתָּה יְיָ אֱלֹהֵינוּ מֶלֶדְ הָעוֹלָם. אֲשֶׁר קִדְּשָׁנוּ בְּמִצְוֹתָיו
וְצִוָּנוּ לְהַדְלִיק נֵר שֶׁל חֲנֻכָּה:

בָּרוּדְ אַתָּה יְיָ אֱלֹהֵינוּ מֶלֶדְ הָעוֹלָם. שֶׁעָשָׂה נִסִּים
לַאֲבוֹתֵינוּ בַּיָּמִים הָהֵם בַּזְּמַן הַזֶּה:

בָּרוּדְ אַתָּה יְיָ אֱלֹהֵינוּ מֶלֶדְ הָעוֹלָם. שֶׁהֶחֱיָנוּ וְקִיְּמָנוּ
וְהִגִּיעָנוּ לַזְּמַן הַזֶּה:

THE JEWISH HOME

Washing the Hands before Eating

Blessed art Thou, O Lord our God, King of the Universe, who hast sanctified us by thy commandments and commanded us concerning the washing of the hands.

בָּרוּדְ אַתָּה יְיָ אֱלֹהֵינוּ מֶלֶדְ הָעוֹלָם. אֲשֶׁר קִדְּשָׁנוּ בְּמִצְוֹתָיו
וְצִוָּנוּ עַל נְטִילַת יָדָיִם:

Grace after Meals

Blessed art thou, O Lord our God, King of the Universe, who feedest the whole world with thy goodness, with grace, with lovingkindness and tender mercy; thou givest food to all flesh, for thy lovingkindness endureth for ever. Through thy great goodness food hath never failed us: O may it not fail us for ever and ever for thy great name's sake, since thou nourishest and sustainest all beings and doest good unto all, and providest food for all thy creatures whom thou hast created. Blessed art Thou, O Lord, who givest food unto all.

(*For complete* "Grace," *see The Standard Prayer Book, Bloch Publishing Co.*)

בָּרוּךְ אַתָּה יְיָ אֱלֹהֵינוּ מֶלֶךְ הָעוֹלָם. הַזָּן אֶת־הָעוֹלָם כֻּלּוֹ. בְּטוּבוֹ בְּחֵן בְּחֶסֶד וּבְרַחֲמִים. הוּא נוֹתֵן לֶחֶם לְכָל־בָּשָׂר. כִּי לְעוֹלָם חַסְדּוֹ: וּבְטוּבוֹ הַגָּדוֹל תָּמִיד לֹא־חָסַר לָנוּ וְאַל יֶחְסַר־לָנוּ מָזוֹן לְעוֹלָם וָעֶד בַּעֲבוּר שְׁמוֹ הַגָּדוֹל. כִּי הוּא זָן וּמְפַרְנֵס לַכֹּל וּמֵטִיב לַכֹּל וּמֵכִין מָזוֹן לְכָל־בְּרִיּוֹתָיו אֲשֶׁר בָּרָא. בָּרוּךְ אַתָּה יְיָ. הַזָּן אֶת־הַכֹּל:

PURIM

Recited before the Reading of the Megillah

Blessed art Thou, O Lord our God, King of the Universe, who hast sanctified us by thy commandments, and hast commanded us concerning the reading of the Megillah.

Blessed art Thou, O Lord our God, King of the Universe, who performed miracles for our fathers in days of old, at this season.

Blessed art Thou, O Lord our God, King of the Universe, who hast kept us in life and hast preserved us, and enabled us to reach this season.

בָּרוּךְ אַתָּה יְיָ אֱלֹהֵינוּ מֶלֶךְ הָעוֹלָם. אֲשֶׁר קִדְּשָׁנוּ בְּמִצְוֹתָיו
וְצִוָּנוּ עַל מִקְרָא מְגִלָּה:

בָּרוּךְ אַתָּה יְיָ אֱלֹהֵינוּ מֶלֶךְ הָעוֹלָם. שֶׁעָשָׂה נִסִּים לַאֲבוֹתֵינוּ
בַּיָּמִים הָהֵם בַּזְּמַן הַזֶּה:

בָּרוּךְ אַתָּה יְיָ אֱלֹהֵינוּ מֶלֶךְ הָעוֹלָם. שֶׁהֶחֱיָנוּ וְקִיְּמָנוּ וְהִגִּיעָנוּ
לַזְּמַן הַזֶּה:

THE FOUR QUESTIONS

(A child recites)

מַה נִּשְׁתַּנָּה הַלַּיְלָה הַזֶּה מִכָּל הַלֵּילוֹת?

שֶׁבְּכָל הַלֵּילוֹת אָנוּ אוֹכְלִין חָמֵץ וּמַצָּה, הַלַּיְלָה הַזֶּה כֻּלּוֹ
מַצָּה.

שֶׁבְּכָל הַלֵּילוֹת אָנוּ אוֹכְלִין שְׁאָר יְרָקוֹת, הַלַּיְלָה הַזֶּה מָרוֹר.

שֶׁבְּכָל הַלֵּילוֹת אֵין אָנוּ מַטְבִּילִין אֲפִילוּ פַּעַם אֶחָת, הַלַּיְלָה
הַזֶּה שְׁתֵּי פְעָמִים.

שֶׁבְּכָל הַלֵּילוֹת אָנוּ אוֹכְלִין בֵּין יוֹשְׁבִין וּבֵין מְסֻבִּין, הַלַּיְלָה
הַזֶּה כֻּלָּנוּ מְסֻבִּין.

(Another child reads the translation)

Why is this night different from all other nights?
On all other nights we eat either leavened or unleavened bread; on this night, why only unleavened?

On all other nights, we eat all kinds of herbs; on
this night, why only bitter herbs?

On all other nights, we do not dip the herbs even
once; why on this night do we dip them twice?

On all other nights, we eat either sitting or leaning;
on this night why do we eat in a leaning position only?

PASSOVER

*(For the complete Seder Service, see Standard Haggadah, **Bloch**
Publishing Co.)*

INDEX

Activities, holiday and school, 30, 44, 62-6, 90, 109, 125, 147-8, 172, 190, 214, 225
Afikomon, 150-1, 155, 159
Ahad Ha'am, 72
Ahasuerus, 127ff
Akiba, Rabbi, 202-3, 205
An Only Kid, 160-1
Antiochus Epiphanes, 96ff
Arabia, 6
Arbor Day, 209
Australia, 39

Babylonia, 195, 200; on calendar, 4
Bar Cochba, 196, 202, 222
Bar Mitzvah, 84, 110ff, 117
Bethar, 196
Bible, 8, 11, 74, et passim
Blessings: grace, 234-5; on bread, 226; on fruit, 227; Hanukah lights, 233-4; honey (Rosh Hashonoh), 227; Purim, before Megillah, 235-6; Rosh Hashonoh candles, 226; Sabbath—candles, 229, children, 229, havdoloh, 231-3, kiddush, 230-1, welcome, 229; Sukkos—in sukkah, 228, over four species, 229; Yom Kippur candles, 227; washing hands, 235
Bokser (St. John's bread), 207-11
Book of Judgment, 218
Book of Life, 24

Calendars, 1ff; solar, lunar, 3
Canaan, 7, 48
China, 39
Christians, 8
Confessional, 35-6
Confirmation, 180ff
Conservative Jews, 11, 28, 185

David, 184
Deuteronomy, 113
Dietary laws, 117ff

Egypt, 151, 220; exodus, 12
Elijah, 81; cup, 160
Esrog, 50, 55ff
Esther, 126ff, 220

Fast of Esther, 200-1
Fast of Gedaliah, 200
Four Questions, 155-6

Galilee, 203, 204
Gateway to Jewish Song, The: Eisenstein, 65
Great White Fast, 34
Greeks and gods, 96ff
Greetings, for New Year, 227

Haftorah, 84, 122
Haggadah, 154, 158, 165-9
Halloween, 141
Haman, 131ff, 220

Hamantaschen, 135
Hamisho Osor B'Shevat, 193, 206ff, 222
Hanukah, 95ff, 219-20; money, 105, 107
Haroses, 152, 157
Havdoloh, 81, 85-6
Hebrew, spoken in Palestine, 141; blessings, 226ff
Heder, 106
High Holidays, 19ff et passim
Hometz, search for, 165-6
Hoshano Rabbo, 58

Iraq, 39

Jerusalem, destruction, 195; Temple, 22 et passim
Jewish National Fund, 179
Jewish Welfare Fund, 105
Josiah, 8
Judah Maccabee, 95ff, 219

Kiddush, 18, 54, 72, 84
Kol Nidre, 34
Kosher, dietary laws, 117ff; for Passover, 164

Lag B'Omer, 193, 201ff, 222
Lamentations, 198-9
Lithuania, 23ff, 78ff, 127, 136, 163ff, 205-6
Lulov, 50, 55ff

Maccabee, 101
Maccabees, Book of the, 98

Mattathias, of Modin, 97, 101, 219
Matzos, 157-8
Mediterranean Sea, 140
Megillah, Book of Esther, 129, 136-7
Menorah, 96, 101, 102, 103, 104, 107, 220
Meron, 203, 204
Mezuzah, 111, 112, 113, 114
Micah, Book of, 27
Modin, 101
Mohammedans, calendar of, 5
Mordecai, 127ff, 220
Moses, 74, 174, 220, 221; Books of, 82
Mount Ararat, 185
Mount Carmel, 185
Mount Hermon, 185
Mount Sinai, 12, 22, 173ff, 184-5
Myrtle, 55ff

Ner Tomid, Eternal Light, 81-2
New Year of the Trees, 207ff
New Year's Eve, 141
N'iloh, 41
Nine Days, 196ff
Noah's Ark, 185

Omer, Counting of, 201-2
Orthodox Jews, 11, 28, 51, 52, 54, 114, 118, 195, 197-8
Orthodox synagogue, 121-2

Palestine, 50, 121, 176-7, 178-9, 200, 207ff, 221; Lag B'Omer, 204; Purim, 139ff; Rosh Hodesh, 10-12; Sabbath, 76-7
Paschal lamb, 157

Passover, 11, 149ff, 176, 220

Pentateuch, 82

Persia, 39, 138

Proverbs, Book of, 69-70

Psalms, 194

Pupil's Activity Book I: Zeligs, 62n

Purim, 126ff, 201; in Palestine, 139ff

Purim-rabbi, 137-8

Reform Jews, 11, 28, 185

Rio de Janeiro, 67

Rock of Ages, 103

Romans, 195-6, 202ff; on calendar, 5

Rosh Hashonoh, 11, 15ff, 68, 200, 217-8

Rosh Hodesh, 8ff, 21, 193-5, 222

Ruth, 184

Sabbath, 21, 33, 67ff, 222-3; blessing children, 71; candles, 69; Sabbath Queen, 77; Sabbath Nachamu, 199; Sabbath sketch, 90-4

Sambatyon, 80

Sanhedrin, on Rosh Hodesh, 9-10

Scholars' Day, 202

Seder, 150ff, 220

Selihos, 25-6

Shalach-mones, 136-7

Shalom Aleihem, chant, 80

Shofar, 20ff, 42

Sh'mini Atzeres, Eighth Day of Solemn Assembly, 59

Shohet, 119

Shovuos, 11, 173ff, 201, 221

Siberia, 39

Simeon bar Yohai, Rabbi, 203ff, 204, 205, 206

Simhas Torah, Rejoicing in the Law, 59-60, 68, 219

Songs of My People: Cooper, 65

Sukkah, 45ff

Sukkos, 7, 11, 45ff, 68, 215, 219

Sun-year, 2

Tablets of the Law, 174

Talis, prayer-shawl, 114-7

Talmud, 11, 12, 207-8

Tammuz, 196; Seventeenth of, 197

Tashlich, 27-8

Tefilin, 114, 117

Tel Aviv, 77, 140ff, 209ff

Temple, 58, 195; rededicated, 100

Ten Commandments, 22, 74, 174-5, 221

Ten Days of Penitence, 24, 218

Thanksgiving Day, 68

Three Books, 23-4

Three Weeks, 196ff

Tishoh B'Ov, 193, 195, 221

Torah, 58; Scrolls, 57, 59, 81, 82-3, 219

Trichinosis, 120

Vashti, 130

Willow, 55ff

Yeshiva, Talmudical college, 137

Yiskor light, 34

Yom Kippur, 10, 19, 20, 31ff, 23, 24, 25, 68, 218

Zohar, 203